You Are Not Powerless

Twelve Steps to Conscious Recovery

A Bold New Approach to Healing Addiction & Depression Through Self-Mastery

Written By:
Jesse J. Jacoby

Copyright ©2025

All rights reserved. No part of this book may be used or reproduced in any manner whatsoever without written permission from the author, with the exception of brief quotations embodied in critical articles, blog posts, or reviews.

Soulspire Publishing
Truckee, CA, 96161

ISBN: 979-8-9900273-9-8
Library of Congress Control Number: 2012921011
Dewey CIP: 641.563   **OCLC:** 213839254

Cover art, font, and layout are all original art by: Jesse J. Jacoby & Abdul Rehman

Wholesalers to book trade: Nelson's Books and Ingram
Available through Amazon.com, BarnesAndNoble.com

Disclaimer

This book is intended for educational and informational purposes only. While the guidance within is supported by professional research, experiential insight, and referenced scientific studies, some of the recommendations may not have been evaluated or approved by the American Medical Association (AMA), the Food and Drug Administration (FDA), or conventional mental health boards at the time of publication.

The content is not meant to substitute professional medical advice, diagnosis, or treatment. Readers are encouraged to consult with a licensed naturopathic doctor, holistic health practitioner, or trusted healthcare provider before making changes to their health regimen, particularly regarding prescription medications, mental health treatments, or medical procedures.

The author disclaims any liability for adverse outcomes or misfortunes that may result from the application of information contained within this work. Each reader assumes full responsibility for their own health and well-being.

Dedication

To my brother, Darin – We only needed a few more years. The answers you were searching for were just beginning to surface. I carry them now, not only for you, but for all those still seeking. May your spirit rest high in the mountains of your longing, finally free.

To my dear friend, Madison – Your presence, your pain, your brilliance still echoes. This book holds your light.

To every beautiful soul, quietly struggling with sadness, despair, and the weight of emotions that feel too heavy to carry – this is for you. You are not alone. You are not powerless.

To all those victimized by the suicide industry – the misdiagnosed, the overmedicated, silenced, I am writing in your honor, and for your liberation.

Lastly, to those who tried to break me – the ones who made my life more difficult, who cast shadows on my path, who tried to make me believe I was not meant to shine – thank you.

When I escaped your hatred, I grew wings. When I slipped through your grip, I began to bloom. When I walked away on my own, I found my destiny. Without discomfort, there is no awakening, and in a world like ours, growth is a rebellion of the spirit.

A Poetic Preface

There is a place the light reaches only after the soul has fallen into deep silence. Where sadness no longer shames us but becomes the fertile ground from which meaning rises.

We have not come here to be broken. We have come here to remember how unbreakable we are when we choose to rise with grace.

To everyone who has ever whispered, *"I cannot do this anymore"* – may these pages speak the voice you needed to hear when the world felt deaf.

This is a ceremony, not a book. A return. A rising. A remembering. You were never meant to carry your despair all alone.

The grief. The pressure. The forgetting of your own magic. You are not the weight that brought you to your knees. You are the prayer that stood back up. The heartbeat beneath the collapse. The hands that still plant seeds in scorched soil.

May you meet yourself here – in these words – not as a problem to fix, but as a mystery to behold. Not as someone behind, but as someone becoming. You are not late. You are right on time.

Allow the heaviness to soften. Let the shame you have been holding dissolve. Receive these lessons as permission to start fresh.

If you forget again – trust that the light will wait for you in the silence. She always does.

Foreword by the Author

As happy as I am today, I admit that life has not always been easy. Even now, I am tested with obstacles and struggles that challenge me to evolve. These trials have reshaped my path countless times. I have been forced to leave careers I once believed in. I had to move away from places where I felt rooted and at peace. I parted ways with relationships I deeply cherished, even when I did not want to. I mourned the loss of loved ones and stood face-to-face with the ache of absence.

I know the feeling of overdrafting a bank account. I know the tight grip of debt. I have even been forcibly exposed to chemicals – stripped of freedom, denied clean water, and deprived of fresh air. These deterrents were not welcomed. I did not ask for them. They came anyway.

Rather than allow them to poison my positivity, I chose to meet them with presence. I did not see them as endpoints. I experienced them as thresholds. Each one held a hidden message, a sacred invitation to begin again. If everything truly happens for a reason, as we are often told, then I intend to unearth the reason behind every challenge that crosses my path. I am empowered by everything.

While I take pride in my uniqueness and the strengths I have gathered through adversity, I know I did not arrive here without hardship. As grateful as I am to have found ways to smile through sorrow, I recognize that not everyone shares this same lens. Many of us feel discontent with who we are or who we have become. Depression has become an epidemic of the spirit, touching too many hearts, too often, in too many silent ways.

In 2022, suicide claimed over 49,000 lives in the United States, averaging one death every eleven minutes. This marked suicide as the eleventh leading cause of death nationwide. Notably, men died by suicide nearly four times more often than women, with white males accounting for approximately sixty-eight percent of these deaths.

I lost my brother, a great mentor, and several friends to suicide over the years. For someone to suffer so deeply that they find the courage to end their own life, this says so much about the intensity of their inner reality. Pain is real and is navigated differently by each of us.

Knowing that millions are yearning for liberation from what weighs them down, I feel a deep responsibility to offer what I have learned. To share what has helped me keep going. Because no matter how dark or bright, life can change in a day. Struggles can become the scaffolding for our highest strength.

The attempt to escape from pain, Dr. Gabor Maté reminds us, *is often what creates more pain.* May these pages offer you a different path – one of courage, presence, and transformation. May they help you move closer to finding what lights you up and enlivens you.

I cannot sit with each of you in person, however, I poured my heart into this book. May this offering be your companion. Let these shared messages encourage action, spark motivation, and guide your path toward self-restoration. You deserve brighter days.

I hope to see you smiling soon.

— Jesse J. Jacoby

The Journey of Conscious Recovery

Opening Chapters
Introduction - 13
The Problem With Conventional Treatment - 14
A Return to Nature: The Ancient Yet Logical Path - 15
What Really Brings Us Down? - 16

The 12 Steps to Conscious Recovery

Step One: Identifying the Culprit - 19
Age & Biological Changes - 20
Family, Social, and Cultural Environment - 21
Gender & Hormonal Imbalances - 21
Genetics & Epigenetics - 22
Chronic Illness & Inflammation - 22
Stress, Life Transitions, and Unprocessed Grief - 23
Medications, Drugs & Hidden Addictions - 24
Self-Perception & Identity Wounds - 24
Trauma Stored in the Body - 25
Who or What is *Your* Culprit? -26

Step Two: Reclaiming Responsibility - 27
The Power of Attitude - 27
Faith Beyond Mental Constructs - 28
Thoughts as Creative Forces - 28

Step Three: Internal Cleansing - 30
Purging Negative Emotions - 30
Living a Chemical-Free Life - 31
Gut, Bowel, and Microbiome Restoration - 32
Natural Detox Tools and Services - 32
Juice Fasting as a Path to Purification - 33
Breath as a Blood Purifier - 34

Step Four: Fueling the Body with Intelligence - 36
Why Organic, Why Now - 37
Raw, Living Foods and Their Biophotons - 37
Understanding Plant-Based Nutrition - 38
Hidden Dangers in Processed Foods & GMOs - 39
Sugar, Gluten, and Inflammatory Culprits - 39
The Forgotten Power of Hydration - 40

Step Five: Reconnecting With Nature & Movement - 43
Grounding & Earth Resonance - 44
Intentional Exercise & Primal Mechanics - 44
Gardening and Soil Contact - 45
Walking Meditations & Outdoor Mindfulness - 46
The Sacred Science of Yoga - 46

Step Six: Cultivating Substance - 48
Discovering Talents and Joyful Expression - 48
Strengthening Character Through Challenge - 49
Lifelong Learning & Mental Expansion - 50
Creating Legacy Through Passion - 50

Step Seven: Purifying Your Sphere of Influence - 52
Conscious Awareness of Influence - 52
Relationships That Elevate - 53
Redefining Success From the Inside Out - 54

Step Eight: Releasing Expectations - 55
Freeing the Mind from Mental Constructs - 55
Detaching From Comparison - 56
Honoring Your Unique Path - 57

Step Nine: Expanding Consciousness - 58
Radical Compassion & Reverence for Life - 58
Practicing True Forgiveness - 59
Grace for Human Mistakes - 60
Acceptance of the Journey - 60

Step Ten: Trusting the Orchestration - 62
Finding Purpose in Pain - 63
From Breakdown to Breakthrough – 64
Everything Has Meaning - 65

Step Eleven: Building a Vision & Action Plan - 67
Reviewing the Foundation - 67
Setting Empowered Intentions - 68
Overcoming Inner Resistance - 69
Becoming the Embodied Version of You - 70

Step Twelve: Becoming the Healer - 72
The GIVE Method - 72
Leading By Example - 73
Mentorship and Sacred Service - 74
Sharing Your Light with the World - 74

Author's Epilogue: The Mirror Speaks Back - 76

Closing Chapters
Living With a New Smile - 78
Creating a Life You Were Meant to Live - 79
The Ripple Effect of Happiness - 81
Awakening the New World Within - 82
A Message to the Future You - 83
The Final Word: Love As Action - 84

About the Author - 89

Bibliography - 90

Introduction

In a world where mental illness is on the rise and depression is at epidemic levels, conventional treatments are failing us. The psychiatric model, often reliant on psychotropic pills and chemical suppression, has not led to healing. If anything, wounds are deepening, fueling rising suicide rates and numbing the spirits of those prescribed.

We have reached the time for a new path, or rather, a return to ancient ways – the paths of nature, wisdom of the body, and intelligence of lifeforce.

This book offers *Twelve Steps to Conscious Recovery* – a bold, holistic, and empowering alternative to the disempowering narrative that claims we are powerless over depression, addiction, or our inner struggles. You are not powerless. You were simply never taught how powerful you really are.

We live in a society overstimulated by artificial frequencies, blue light, and constant digital noise. The rise of smart technologies, while convenient, has silently contributed to melancholy and mental fragmentation. In contrast, we also have tools – frequency-based healing, Rife technology, grounding, and breathwork – that can sweep away the energetic debris.

Many modern diseases of the mind have roots in the gut. Bowel toxins, candida overgrowth, and harmful microbes can trigger states of confusion, anxiety, and even psychosis. Nature offers answers: polyphenols, pigments, raw juices, and antioxidants which work to purify the blood and restore clarity. Detoxification is the ancient art of self-liberation; this is not merely a trend.

Chemical exposure, nutritional depletion, sedentarism, and emotional suppression have become silent architects of depression. These factors can easily be reversed. Through movement, breath, and reclaiming our personal agency, we can rebuild our nervous systems and awaken joy.

This is a call to rise, not just a book about healing. May this serve as a reminder to take your life back from those who profit from pain. These guidelines are encouraging you to become an indestructible, sovereign being.

These twelve steps are not based on powerlessness, but on your inherent strength. They do not ask you to submit to a higher power outside of you, but to discover the sacred order within you.

Welcome to a new paradigm. One rooted in nature, in truth, and in the unshakeable belief that you were born to heal. Now we begin.

The Problem with Conventional Treatment

"Everything you can imagine is real." — Pablo Picasso

For fourteen years, a poster hung above my desk where I researched and completed writings that featured a Buddha quote: *"Your mind is what creates this world."* Behind the words, a window opens to the mountains of Tibet. This image always reminded me: we create the world we live in through our thoughts, actions, and energy. When our thoughts remain stagnant, our outer world follows. If we choose to believe we are stuck, powerless, or broken – we will continue to experience this reality.

This understanding aligns with the Law of Attraction. What we focus on expands. When our attention dwells on lack, pain, sadness, or addiction, we unconsciously magnetize more of those experiences into our lives. True recovery begins by shifting this focus. Not toward denial, but in the direction of deliberate transformation.

Unfortunately, most conventional treatments do not acknowledge this truth. Psychiatric approaches often center on labels and chemical suppression. Rehabs are structured around narratives of powerlessness, with participants repeating phrases like, *"I am powerless over my addiction."* No substance holds power unless we give away power, and no diagnosis defines the totality of who we are.

Imagine entering a treatment program where the daily conversation revolves around addiction, relapse, triggers, and pathology. Couple that with nutrient-deficient food, no exercise, fluorescent lights, and an absence of creativity or purpose. What kind of healing can happen there? Now add prescription drugs – many with side effects like anxiety, depression, or suicidal thoughts – and you have a system designed to manage dysfunction, not create well-being.

According to recent studies, antidepressant use among young people has escalated significantly. Between January 2016 and December 2022, the monthly antidepressant dispensing rate for U.S. adolescents and young adults aged twelve to twenty-five years increased by 66.3%. Despite this surge in medication use, suicide rates have continued to rise. In 2022, approximately 49,476 individuals died by suicide in the United States, equating to an age-adjusted rate of 14.2 per 100,000 people. This trend suggests that current treatment approaches may not be effectively addressing the underlying issues contributing to mental health crises.

What if, instead, we reimagined recovery as a process of remembering who we truly are? A journey of nourishment, movement, purpose, and connection. What if rehab looked like time in nature, plant-based meals, breathwork, education, and building a meaningful life path? What if therapy focused not only on pain but on possibility? What if we were encouraged to dwell on our strengths, vision, and joy, rather than rehearsing wounds of the past?

This is what Conscious Recovery is about. The approach is not pharmaceutical, or a forever identity rooted in diagnosis. This is a call to rise.

This book does not deny suffering but refuses to make suffering your identity. Here, you will not be asked to repeat that you are powerless. You will be reminded that you are potent and that the path to healing is not through sedation – but through awakening.

Let these Twelve Steps guide you – not into management of dysfunction – but into mastery of self.

A Return to Nature: The Ancient, Logical Path

"When the world becomes too loud, find the forest within."

True healing is remembered, this is not something new. Long before pharmaceutical companies, before psychiatry, and before dependency became a business model, humans healed through communion with nature, through rhythm, breath, plants, silence, sweat, and story. This path is still here. The tools have simply been buried beneath the noise.

We do not lack solutions. We are lacking reconnection. The modern world is built on acceleration, yet the soul thrives in stillness. This explains why anxiety and depression are on the rise while our connection to the natural world is in decline. The moment we return to nature – both around us and within us – we begin to remember our original intelligence. We remember that healing is intuitive. That health is a lifestyle. That joy is not a chemical but a state of coherence.

Happiness and health are not destinations we achieve through material gain or intellectual success. They are byproducts of harmony – between mind and body, spirit and soil, breath and being.

To access this harmony, we must subtract what does not belong: toxic foods, toxic thoughts, and toxic environments. We are required to return to the logic of our ancestors who knew that clean water, sunlight, fresh air, vibrant food, spiritual practice, movement, and community were the foundations of a thriving life.

Many people say they are happy but have not yet tasted what real vitality feels like. When your blood is clean, your gut is thriving, and your nervous system is calm, your baseline happiness elevates. True health unlocks a form of joy that radiates and is not conditional.

What Really Brings Us Down?

"We do not see things as they are, we see them as we are." — Anaïs Nin

Millions of people today are seeking freedom from depression, but many are placing their trust in the wrong solutions. Reliance on antidepressants has skyrocketed, especially among women in midlife. Yet what is often marketed as a cure is, in truth, a chemical bandage – masking symptoms, deepening dependency, and evading true healing.

One in four women between the ages of forty and fifty-nine in the U.S. is taking an antidepressant. We have been conditioned to view depression as a mysterious disease with no cure, but this belief is more disabling than the condition.

"There is only one cause of unhappiness: The false beliefs we have in our head. Beliefs so widespread, so commonly held, that we never question them." — Anthony de Mello

Sometimes we carry grief. In other instances, we are traumatized. Often, our daily choices – the food we consume, our thoughts, our level of movement, and our environment – have the greatest influence over how we feel.

We stay in toxic relationships. We eat food that robs our energy. We neglect nature. We absorb chemicals. We feel powerless in jobs that underpay us. We stay silent when our hearts long to speak.

If we want to heal, we must identify what is truly bringing us down – and act. First, let's examine the most accepted causes of depression. These are the often-ignored roots of depression, and they are reversible:

Antagonist List (What We Have Been Told)

- Age (Elderly at higher risk)
- Biology (Monoamine theory of depression)
- Family & Social Environment (Abuse, poverty)
- Gender (Women are twice as likely to be depressed)
- Genetics (Runs in families)
- Health Conditions (Cancer, Heart Disease, Obesity)
- Life Changes & Stress (Divorce, financial hardship)
- Substance Use & Medications (Prescriptions)
- Negative Self-Image (Appearance, fear of rejection)
- Trauma & Grief (Loss, injury, heartbreak)

These are the conventional scapegoats. While they reflect real pain, many are rooted in things we are told we cannot change – such as our age, gender, or genes. What if this is only part of the story? What if we have far more power than we have been led to believe?

Protagonist List (What Is Within Our Control)

- Physical inactivity
- Poor diet and processed foods
- A synthetic, disconnected environment
- Over-reliance on pharmaceutical medications
- Repressed emotions and unprocessed trauma
- Negative thinking patterns and pessimism
- Living by others' expectations
- Lack of purpose or passion
- Intellectual stagnation
- Toxic social circles
- Lack of compassion and empathy
- Inaction, procrastination, and fear of change
- Disconnection from nature
- Gut imbalance and harmful microbes

As we begin this journey, I encourage you to examine which of these are showing up in your life. Are you holding onto someone else's expectations? Do you spend your days surrounded by lifeless food, stale routines, or artificial environments? Are you hydrated, or is your brain running on fumes? Are your emotions being processed or suppressed? Your answers matter.

The truth is: depression is largely sedentary in nature and healing is inherently active. When we move – physically, emotionally, intellectually, spiritually – we open space for joy. Whether walking in the sun, learning a new skill, expressing our creativity, or simply breathing deeply, each act of engagement chips away at despair.

We do not require more diagnoses. We are longing for more vitality. We seek laughter. We need real food, real purpose, and real connection.

Most people are not depressed because of a genetic defect. They are overcast because they are disconnected – from nature, from purpose, from movement, from their breath, from meaningful relationships. This is what we are here to claim.

You are not broken. You are blocked. Blocks can be cleared. Let this chapter be your invitation to take full ownership of your energy, your choices, your food, your thoughts, and your joy.

In the steps ahead, we will identify what has dimmed your light and show you how to rise, radiantly.

"Most of the shadows of this life are caused by standing in our own sunshine." — Ralph Waldo Emerson

Step One: Identifying the Culprit
Uncovering the Root Causes

"Whatever happens to you, do not fall in despair. Even if all the doors are closed, a secret path will be there for you that no one knows." — Rumi

Before healing can begin, we must first uncover the source of our pain. This step invites us to identify the true culprits behind our sadness, despair, or disconnection – not the ones we have been taught to accept without question, but those hidden in plain sight. While modern mental health narratives often encourage us to believe we are helpless victims of age, biology, or misfortune, this step urges us to dig deeper. The truth reveals that we are not broken, we are blocked.

Too often, we have allowed the world to convince us that our suffering stems from things we cannot control. Our age. Our genetics. Our hormones. What if we are looking in the wrong direction? What if the path to happiness requires us to stop blaming and start reclaiming?

This is about sacred accountability – the kind that reclaims power from the places we unknowingly gave away. Our healing begins not when someone else saves us, but when we become curious enough to listen inward. To lean into discomfort. To witness our lives with new eyes.

In this first step, we do not label ourselves – we liberate. We gather our scattered truths and hold them like seeds, knowing that awareness is the first spark of transformation.

The Twelve Steps to Conscious Recovery begin with radical honesty. This step is about identifying the influences, experiences, and habits that have shaped our suffering and acknowledging that we have the power to shift them.

Over the next pages, we will walk through ten areas of life that are often misunderstood as root causes of depression. Together, we will shed light on what really brings us down and reveal the empowering truth behind each of these culprits:

- Age & Biological Changes
- Family, Social, and Cultural Environment
- Gender & Hormonal Imbalances
- Genetics & Epigenetics
- Chronic Illness & Inflammation
- Stress, Life Transitions, and Unprocessed Grief
- Medications, Drugs & Hidden Addictions
- Self-Perception & Identity Wounds
- Trauma Stored in the Body
- Who or What is Your Culprit?

By reading through each of these, you will be invited to assess your personal landscape with curiosity and courage. You will notice patterns. You will start connecting your emotional and physical state to the foods you eat, thoughts you think, and the environments you inhabit.

The goal of Step One is to uncover, not to shame. To illuminate, not to punish. Once we know what is holding us back, we can release. When we let go of this energy that does not serve us, we create space for what does.

Now we begin with awareness. This discernment leads to change. Metamorphosis begins here, with you.

Age & Biological Changes

"Count your age by friends, not years. Count your life by smiles, not tears." — John Lennon

Age is not a cause of depression, stagnation is. As we age, we are often told that decline is inevitable. That our best days are behind us. The truth is, we do not get old because we age, we get old when our fluids stagnate and we stop growing, moving, nourishing, and evolving.

Yes, statistics show that older adults are more prone to depression. Behind the numbers, patterns are clear: as we age, we tend to become more sedentary. We may retire, reduce social interaction, eat more processed foods, or rely more heavily on medications with depressive side effects. This lifestyle is the culprit.

There is another way. There are vibrant elders around the world thriving into their 70s, 80s, and 90s. They are primarily plant-based, active, and joy-filled. People like Mimi Kirk, Jim Morris, and Karyn Calabrese are living proof that age can be a celebration, not a sentence.

Biologically, depression is often attributed to *"chemical imbalances,"* but this oversimplifies a much more complex system. Your biology is responsive. You are shaped by what you eat, how you breathe, how you move, and how you think. Clean foods, rich in polyphenols and antioxidants, support the nervous system and regulate neurotransmitters naturally. Movement improves brain chemistry. Meditation reduces inflammation. Nature restores balance.

Your cells are listening to everything you believe. So, what if you believed that aging could be vibrant, expansive, and sacred? You are not too old to heal. You are not too young to rise. Wherever you are, your vitality begins with your choices.

Family, Social, and Cultural Environment

"You are not what happened to you but what you choose to become." — Carl Jung

We do not get to choose the family or community we are born into. Some of us arrive at love and safety. Others with chaos, conflict, poverty, or violence. These early environments shape how we view ourselves and the world, but they do not define us.

Yes, abuse, neglect, and poverty each leave scars. A toxic household, an unsafe neighborhood, or a culture that limits your potential can shake your sense of worth. If any of these conditions planted the seed of sorrow, this book offers you the tools to cultivate a new soil. One rich in nourishment, support, and possibility.

Your environment affects your health more than you may realize. Poor food access, chronic stress, environmental toxins, and social isolation all contribute to depression. But here is the good news: community can also be a cure. Gardens can be planted. Healthy food systems can be built. Support can be found. Inspiration can be shared.

The stories of Ron Finley, Will Allen, and others who transformed impoverished neighborhoods with urban gardens are proof that we are never without power. When you bring life back to the soil, you bring life back to the soul.

Even if your past environment taught you pain, you can choose a new path now. You can seek mentors, join communities, reconnect with nature, and create beauty in places where this never felt possible. You are not your upbringing. You are not your zip code. You are the architect of your next chapter.

Gender & Hormonal Imbalances

"Balance is something you create, not find."

Much has been made about the connection between gender and depression. Statistically, women are more likely to report depression, while men are more likely to suffer in silence or act out in ways that mask their pain. Beneath the statistics lies a truth we must all face: imbalance – whether hormonal, emotional, or energetic – can disrupt our joy.

Yes, hormones influence mood. Shifts in estrogen, progesterone, and testosterone affect brain chemistry. These shifts are not the problem. The issue lies in what we feed our bodies, how we handle stress, and how disconnected we have become from the rhythms of nature.

Birth control, synthetic hormones, processed foods, dairy, and chronic stress can wreak havoc on endocrine function. For men and women alike, hormonal imbalance often emerges from inflammatory foods, exposure to xenoestrogens (chemical hormone disruptors), sleep deprivation, and emotional suppression. We are not powerless to these effects. Through plant-based nutrition, breathwork, detoxification, liver support, adaptogenic herbs, and emotional clearing, balance can be restored.

You are not at war with your biology. Your body is your ally. Whether you are navigating menstruation, menopause, or male hormonal decline, the key is alignment – not fear. Wholeness comes not from perfection, but from presence. Let us step into this chapter with reverence for our bodies, compassion for our experiences, and the conviction that balance is not beyond us, but is within reach.

Genetics & Epigenetics

"Genetics may load the gun, but lifestyle pulls the trigger." — Dr. Caldwell Esselstyn

For decades, we have been told that our genes determine our destiny. If depression, *"runs in the family",* we are expected to accept this as fate. This narrative is outdated and disempowering. While genetics play a role, they are not the final word. The science of epigenetics reveals a more hopeful truth: we can influence how our genes express themselves.

Your DNA is a script, not a sentence. Scripts can be rewritten. Through your daily choices – what you eat, how you move, how you think, and how you love – you are constantly signaling your genes. A nutrient-rich, plant-based diet; regular movement; adequate sleep; and a mind rooted in gratitude can turn off inflammatory genes and activate ones that support health, vitality, and emotional balance.

The foods we inherit from our families often mirror the diseases we inherit. So, when someone says, *"this runs in the family,"* what is often running is the same toxic diet, same stress patterns, and same disconnection from nature. Often, nobody in the family runs or is exercising.

You can break the cycle. You have the potential to be the one in your family who rewrites the story – not just for yourself, but for future generations. Epigenetics show us that healing does not stop with us, our decision to clean up our cells and genetic imprints ripples forward.

Let this be your reminder: You are not a victim of your biology. You are the author of your healing.

Chronic Illness & Inflammation

"Inflammation is the root of all disease but does not have to be the root of your story."

Living with a chronic illness is difficult. This infliction can limit your movement, cloud your mind, drain your energy, and make each day feel like a mountain. When you are constantly managing pain or symptoms, your chances of slipping into despair broaden. What if we understand these conditions not as life sentences – but as signals?

Conditions like diabetes, obesity, heart disease, autoimmune disorders, and even depression often share a common origin: chronic inflammation. This is your body's cry for balance, for nourishment, for change.

The root causes of inflammation hide in plain sight: processed food, clarified sugar, dairy, tap water, sedentary living, environmental toxins, unresolved emotions, and a disconnection from nature. The solution is equally close: hydration, whole foods, detoxification, movement, and self-compassion.

Even if you have received a diagnosis, or if you have been told there is no cure, there is always something you can do. Thousands of people have reversed their symptoms, and lives, by removing inflammatory triggers and embracing a more vibrant way of living.

Plant-based diets, juicing, fasting, lymphatic movement, emotional release practices, and gut restoration have all shown powerful results. Healing begins when we stop fighting our bodies and start listening to them.

You are not defined by your condition. You are not the label. You are not stuck. Perfection is also not required to begin adjusting. You simply need to be willing to believe that healing is possible and take the first step.

Stress, Life Transitions, & Unprocessed Grief

"Grief is a portal to depth, to healing, to a more compassionate life – not a sign of weakness." — Francis Weller

Life is not linear. Our experience comes in seasons, chapters, and waves. Sometimes, without warning, everything changes. A relationship ends, a job is lost, or someone we love passes away. Even joyful events like moving to a new city, becoming a parent, or changing careers can leave us reeling.

In a culture that glorifies constant productivity, we are rarely given permission to grieve or to slow down and recalibrate. Yet unresolved grief is one of the most common undercurrents beneath depression. This lives in the body, waiting to be witnessed, honored, and released.

Stress is a signal that is not inherently bad. A messenger calling for rest, reflection, or transformation – that when ignored – builds. Chronic stress triggers inflammation, disrupts digestion, floods our systems with cortisol, and rewires our perception toward fear and survival.

The remedy is not to eliminate all stress or avoid all change. The solution is to become resourced – mentally, emotionally, and spiritually. Practices like breathwork, journaling, nature immersion, and nervous system regulation help us metabolize life's intensity rather than suppress.

Grief is an emotion to feel, not an illness to fix. Life transitions are not punishments. They are initiations. In their unraveling, we often meet a more honest version of ourselves. Let this be your reminder: You are allowed to mourn, to pause, to heal. You are allowed to begin again.

Medications, Drugs & Hidden Addictions

"Addiction is about the disconnection, not the substance." — Dr. Gabor Maté

We live in a culture of quick fixes – where discomfort is numbed rather than understood, and prescriptions are handed out more readily than compassion. Whether alcohol, antidepressants, stimulants, sedatives, or illicit substances, many turn to chemistry to escape the complexity of emotion.

The truth is: *what we medicate, we often fail to heal.* While certain medications may offer temporary relief or be *necessary* in specific cases, they are not cures. They alter brain chemistry and can lead to dependency, emotional dullness, or long-term health complications. Likewise, alcohol and recreational drugs may bring short-term relief – but they often mask deeper needs: for connection, purpose, pleasure, rest, or love.

Addiction of any kind – subtle or extreme – is a symptom of unmet needs and unprocessed pain. Rather than labeling ourselves as powerless, we are invited to get curious. What void are we trying to fill? What pain are we trying to silence?

Gut-brain connection is vital here. Many medications and substances harm our microbiome, disrupting the balance that supports serotonin production, immune health, and mood regulation. Healing addiction, therefore, involves more than willpower. This requires replenishing the body, releasing the pain, and finding joy again.

Detoxification, nutrient repletion, community support, emotional healing, movement, and purpose – these all play a role in sustainable recovery. You are not powerless. You are powerful beyond belief. You do not need to fight addiction – you need to remember who you are beneath.

Self-Perception & Identity Wounds

"How you see yourself determines how you move."

Many people walk through life believing they are not enough. Not attractive enough, not smart enough, not strong enough, not worthy enough. This deep inner wound, often rooted in childhood experiences or cultural programming, becomes the silent architect of depression.

When we internalize rejection, criticism, or comparison, we start living in a narrative that was never ours to begin with. We dim our light to fit in. We shrink to avoid standing out. Over time, this erodes our joy.

The good news? Identity is not fixed. Self-perception can be rewritten. The process of healing begins the moment we stop asking the world for permission to love ourselves.

The most beautiful transformations happen when we stop trying to be someone else's version of acceptable and start becoming our own definition of whole.

You are not your weight. You are not your scars. You are not your past. You are a dynamic being capable of rewriting your beliefs, reconnecting with your brilliance, and remembering that your worth is not conditional.

This step invites you to look in the mirror – not to critique, but to meet yourself with curiosity. What have you been taught to believe about who you are? What old narratives are asking to be released? Reclaim your self-image as sacred. Begin to nourish your inner landscape with thoughts, foods, and actions that honor the truth of who you really are. You are enough. You always were. Keep going.

Trauma Stored in the Body

"Your body remembers everything – even the things your mind has tried to forget."

Not all trauma is loud. Some whisper through tight shoulders, clenched jaws, shallow breaths, and restless sleep. Trauma embedded in our tissues, nervous system, and fascia – when left unprocessed – can even manifest as depression, anxiety, numbness, or chronic pain.

In the wild, animals instinctively release trauma by shaking vigorously after a life-threatening event. This primal discharge is the nervous system's way of returning to balance. They move through, rather than intellectualizing the threat. They literally shake off potential trauma. Humans, however, have largely forgotten this natural response. Instead of moving trauma through the body, we often freeze, tighten, suppress, and store. The result? Fragmentation. Postural tension. Emotional disconnection.

Somatic practices that imitate this shaking – such as TRE (Tension & Trauma Releasing Exercises), dance therapy, and rebound movement – can help our bodies complete the cycle that nature intended.

Additionally, biohacking technologies like vibration plate therapy and PEMF (Pulsed Electromagnetic Field) therapy offer powerful ways to support the body's release of stored trauma. Vibration plates stimulate lymphatic flow, fascia release, and muscular activation, helping to physically dislodge stored stress. PEMF helps re-regulate electrical signaling in the body, calming the nervous system and enhancing cellular repair. These tools, when used mindfully, can amplify the work of natural healing and reconnect us to our innate vitality.

You do not have to relive trauma to heal – but you are required to acknowledge the presence. Your body is the keeper of your story, waiting patiently for you to listen.

Somatic healing, breathwork, yoga, EMDR, journaling, and energy work are powerful ways to move trauma through and out of the body. What was once stuck can become fluid. What once felt heavy can be released. What once felt like a wound can become a window.

Do not carry the weight of old pain forever. There is wisdom beneath the wounds. There is freedom on the other side of feeling. You are safe now.

Who or What is Your Culprit?

"You cannot heal what you will not name."

Now that we have uncovered hidden influences behind depression, we can turn the spotlight inward. Of the ten areas explored – age, hormones, trauma, health, addiction, and more – where do you most feel a resonance? What sections stirred something in you? Which ones made you pause and reflect?

This final section of Step One is your opportunity to integrate and clarify. To get honest about what is really bringing you down – not to judge, but to empower yourself.

Maybe you are experiencing a mix of several culprits. Maybe there is one you have been afraid to face. Whatever this may be, acknowledge the presence, sit with the reality, and write out your solutions. Ask yourself: *What is within my control to change? What is within my power to release? What do I need to embrace to feel lighter, clearer, freer?*

You are not the story you inherited. You are not the symptoms you have been managing. You are not the label someone gave you. You are an evolving, powerful being capable of healing, rising, and rewriting your path.

Step Two: Reclaiming Responsibility

The Shift from Reaction to Creation

"Correcting oneself is correcting the whole world. The sun is simply bright and does not correct anyone. Because of this perpetual shine, the world is full of light." — Ramana Maharshi

Having named the culprits behind our despair, we now take a brave and empowering step forward: we reclaim responsibility. Not blame, but response-ability – the ability to consciously respond, rather than unconsciously react.

This step is about choosing what is possible, not fixing what is broken. We begin to redirect energy from analyzing what went wrong to creating what could be right. We take the scattered puzzle pieces of pain and use them to shape a new vision. This all begins with our attitude.

To reclaim responsibility is to reclaim authorship of your life. This is the moment we stop waiting for someone else to apologize, to change, to rescue us – and instead begin the quiet, powerful work of transformation from within. We do not deny injustice or excuse harm; we choose not to let pain write our story. We become the narrator again.

Many people carry silent agreements with powerlessness. These contracts were often signed in childhood, in environments where control, choice, or voice were stripped away. What was once survival no longer serves our evolution. This step is a sacred revision. A chance to say: I am no longer helpless. I am the healer now. The architect. The bridge.

Gabor Maté writes, *"When we are not conscious, we do not respond to life – we react."* This step is an invitation to awaken the part of you that can pause, breathe, and choose. To move from reflex to reflection. From conditioned story to conscious creation. In that space, you begin to build a different life – not from scarcity or shame, but from soul.

The Power of Attitude

"There is very little difference in people, but that little difference makes a big difference. The little difference is attitude." — W. Clement Stone

Two people can experience the same hardship and emerge in radically different ways. One grows bitter. The other grows wiser. What makes the difference? Attitude.

Attitude is the lens through which we interpret the world – coloring our thoughts, choices, and our resilience. A positive attitude does not mean toxic optimism or denial but choosing to orient ourselves toward solutions, gratitude, and growth.

Viktor Frankl, who survived the horrors of a concentration camp, reminds us that *"everything can be taken from a man but one thing: the last of the human freedoms – to choose one's attitude in any given set of circumstances."*

Your attitude is your inner compass which determines whether you give up or rise. Whether you shrink or shine. Whether you spiral into despair or stretch into evolution. When we reclaim our attitude, we reclaim our direction.

Faith Beyond Mental Constructs

"Nature loves courage. You make the commitment and nature will respond." — Terence McKenna

Mental faith is conscious alignment, not blind belief. This is defined as a knowing that something greater is at work, and that you are not separate. Faith bridges the space between where you are and where you long to be.

Many people lack mental faith because they have been taught to expect disappointment. They have forgotten that belief precedes transformation. Once you believe – even a little – that change is possible, life rushes in to meet you.

Faith is also trust in your own intuition – believing that your inner compass knows how to guide you, even if you cannot see the whole map. Whether your faith is spiritual, creative, or grounded in nature, this must continue to be nourished. The moment you trust the whisper inside you; this speaks louder.

You are not here to be ruled by fear. You are here to become fluent in the language of trust. Trust in your body. Trust in the path. Trust in your power to shape your world.

Thoughts as Creative Forces

"You are what your deep, driving desire is. As your desire is, so is your will. As your will is, so is your deed. As your deed is, so is your destiny." — Upanishads

Your thoughts are not background noise. They are brushstrokes painting your reality. Each one carries frequency. Each one shapes the way your nervous system responds to life.

A thought held long enough becomes a belief. A belief practiced long enough becomes a behavior. Behavior, when repeated long enough, becomes a life.

This is why healing begins with awareness. Begin to watch your thoughts. Not to judge them, but to understand them. Are they rooted in fear or in possibility? Are they replaying the past or rehearsing the future you desire?

Plant new thoughts like seeds. Affirm what is true and life-giving. Water them with gratitude. Give them light through loving action. Soon, they will bloom.

To reclaim responsibility is to reclaim the pen. You are the author now. The story is still being written. In this new chapter, you are no longer a character reacting to the plot, you are the one shaping how all unfolds.

Step Three: Internal Cleansing

Clear the Vessel

"To bring happiness to others, we must be happiness. To be happiness, we must care for our own bodies and minds." — Thich Nhat Hanh

Cleansing is a sacred return, not a trend. We remember how to care for the vessel that carries our spirit. If the body is the garden of the soul, then cleansing is the tending, the pulling of weeds, the watering of roots. In Step Three, we return to our internal landscape, and we begin to clear.

This is not about punishment or restrictions. This is about liberation. We liberate the gut from stagnation, the blood from toxicity, the brain from fog, and the heart from suppressed emotion. We clear what clouds our perception, dulls our intuition, and dims our light.

Soulspire: The Healing Playground, with locations in Truckee and Nevada City, California, offers a full spectrum of cleansing and biohacking protocols – from colon hydrotherapy and PEMF therapy to infrared sauna, lymphatic massage, and juice fasting. These are not luxuries. These are tools of deep renewal, pathways to vitality. This is the moment to clear the vessel.

In this step, we explore:

- Purging Negative Emotions
- Living a Chemical-Free Life
- Gut, Bowel, and Microbiome Restoration
- Natural Detox Tools and Services
- Juice Fasting as a Path to Purification

Purging Negative Emotions

"Anger is an acid that can do more harm to the vessel in which stored than to anything on which poured." — Mark Twain

Negative emotions are energetic messengers, not moral failings. If we do not listen, they do not disappear. They settle in our tissues, gut, posture, and perception of life. Cleansing the body is not just about physical waste. We also target energetic waste – the suppressed grief, buried rage, unspoken sadness. These emotions create biochemical shifts that alter our pH, disrupt our microbiome, and influence neurotransmitter balance. They become part of the terrain unless we consciously release them.

In Traditional Chinese Medicine, each organ holds an emotion. The liver stores anger, lungs hold grief, and the kidneys fear. As we cleanse the physical body, we also open emotional channels. Through breathwork, cold plunges, movement, prayer, sauna, sound healings, and tears we give the emotions permission to move.

Letting go is honing strength to become soft again; this is not weakness. Science confirms this, too. The gut-brain axis shows us how emotional regulation is linked to microbial diversity. An inflamed gut can mean an inflamed mood. When we fast, when we hydrate, when we remove inflammatory foods and chemical irritants – we calm the system. We lighten the emotional load.

As we detoxify physically, we begin to rewire ourselves emotionally. We may notice forgiveness coming easier. To feel joy. To breathe more deeply. To move through the world with a little less armor.

You are not your emotions. You are the sky that holds the weather. Let them pass through. Let the cleansing begin.

Living a Chemical-Free Life

"The greatest threat to our health is not what we know but what we do not know we are consuming every day."

We are exposed to more chemicals in a single day than our ancestors encountered in a lifetime. From the food we eat to the products we apply to our skin, from the water we drink to the air we breathe, our modern environment is saturated with synthetic toxins. The body is resilient but is not invincible.

To live chemical-free is to live awake. We reclaim sovereignty over our choices, homes, and bodies. Choosing purity represents awareness. What we put on, and in our bodies, becomes part of our blood, breath, and ultimately, our state of mind. Start by purifying your kitchen. Eliminate processed foods, artificial sweeteners, flavor enhancers, dyes, preservatives, and anything that comes with a long list of unpronounceable ingredients. Switch to organic produce. Filter your water. Read labels. Less packaging, more life.

Then shift your attention to your bathroom cabinet. Toothpaste, deodorant, shampoo, lotion, makeup, sunscreen – nearly all conventional personal care products are laced with parabens, phthalates, sulfates, and other endocrine-disrupting chemicals. These compounds accumulate in fat cells, inflame the nervous system, and disrupt hormonal harmony.

Seek out earth-based alternatives. Plant oils. Herbal tonics. Clay, charcoal, and vinegar. Let your skin breathe. Let your body detox. Let your home become a healing space, not a chemical storm.

Chemical exposure also calcifies the pineal gland – the seat of intuition and melatonin production. A foggy pineal means a foggy mind. To decalcify this sacred gland, avoid fluoride and opt for distilled or spring water. Add minerals back in with lemon, cucumber, or trace mineral drops.

Remember: detoxification is not a single act but a commitment to a lifestyle. When we align our choices with purity, the body rewards us. Clarity returns. Energy expands. Joy becomes our baseline. To live chemical-free is to return to what is real.

Gut, Bowel, and Microbiome Restoration

"All disease begins in the gut." — Hippocrates

Long before the science of probiotics or microbiome mapping, ancient healers knew that vitality lives in the gut. Today, research confirms what wisdom has always known: *the state of your microbiome shapes the state of your mind.*

The human gut is home to trillions of microbes – bacteria, fungi, viruses – all communicating with your brain through the vagus nerve. They influence how you digest, how you think, and how you feel. A healthy gut produces more serotonin than the brain does. When your microbiome thrives, your mood follows.

In modern life, this delicate ecosystem is under siege. Antibiotics, processed foods, glyphosate-laced produce, chronic stress, and environmental toxins all contribute to dysbiosis – a disruption of microbial balance that can lead to anxiety, depression, fatigue, and inflammation.

Internal cleansing, colon hydrotherapy, kambo, and biohacking tools like PEMF and Rife frequency help restore gut integrity. What you feed your gut afterward is also important. Fermented foods (like sauerkraut, coconut kefir, and kimchi), prebiotic fiber (found in plants) and high-quality plant-based probiotics begin the rebuilding.

At *Soulspire*, microbiome repair is a foundation of emotional and physical restoration. Through programs combining functional nutrition, colon hydrotherapy, ozone therapy, and advanced gut healing protocols, clients begin to experience life in a body that feels clean, light, and emotionally stable.

As you restore your gut, you are also restoring your joy. Your microbiome is a landscape of mood, resilience, and intuition, not just physical terrain. We are directed to tend to the health of our gut with reverence and intention.

Natural Detox Tools and Services

"The body is a source of vast intelligence. Our task is to listen, support, and create the conditions for natural healing."

In a world brimming with stimulation and synthetic inputs, our bodies are bombarded daily with toxins – chemical, emotional, and energetic. Detoxification is about re-alignment, not deprivation. This is a homecoming.

Natural detox tools are like tuning forks for the body, each one helping you recalibrate back to your most vibrant frequency. At Soulspire, we use an integrative model that blends ancient purification rituals with modern biohacking science. Clients experience cleansing protocols that reawaken cellular intelligence and remove stagnation from the lymph, skin, colon, and brain.

Some of the most effective detox tools include:

- **Colon hydrotherapy**: A gentle and deeply effective method to remove old waste, gas, and microbial residue from the large intestine. This not only supports digestion but also lightens the mental and emotional load.
- **Steam sauna**: By inducing a deep, cellular sweat, steam therapy helps the body release heavy metals, chemicals, and stored trauma.
- **Lymphatic drainage massage**: The lymph system, unlike blood, has no pump and relies on movement. Manual stimulation via massage or vibration plate therapy helps move stagnant lymph and clear metabolic waste.
- **PEMF therapy**: Pulsed Electromagnetic Field therapy recharges cells, boosts mitochondrial function, and restores electrical balance of tissues. Think of cellular reawakening.
- **Oxygen therapy**: In the form of ozone baths or hyperbaric chambers, oxygen floods the cells, starves pathogens, and revitalizes the body at the core.
- **Rebounding and movement-based cleansing**: Gentle exercises like rebounding on a mini trampoline stimulate the lymph and circulation, enhancing detox pathways naturally.
- **Kambo therapy**: An ancient Amazonian practice involving the secretion of the *Phyllomedusa bicolor* frog, applied through small burns on the skin. Though intense, Kambo is revered for deep purgative effects – cleansing the liver, lymph, and gut, while often catalyzing powerful emotional release. Many describe feeling a heightened connection to their body, sharper intuition, and a sense of spiritual clarity. For some, this is a sacred doorway to renewal.

These therapies are not band-aids. They are invitations to activate the brilliance of the body and begin self-repair. The more we detox, the more we feel. The more we feel, the more we come home to our true selves.

We can now move into one of the most powerful detox methods available: juice fasting.

Juice Fasting as a Path to Purification

"Fasting is a spiritual feast, not just a physical discipline."

Of all the ways to cleanse, few are as ancient or effective as the fast. Juice fasting is a sacred pause – a moment to let the body rest, mind reset, and spirit rise.

When we fast, we interrupt the constant influx of digestion and give our system space to redirect energy toward repair. The gut takes a breath. The liver gets to sort and release. The cells begin to regenerate. The body heals.

Juice fasting allows us to nourish while we detox. Cold-pressed, organic juices made from vibrant fruits and vegetables offer a flood of hydration, antioxidants, polyphenols, and plant intelligence – all without the burden of fiber or digestion.

What we remove from our consumption during the fast is equally as important: inflammatory foods, stimulants, chemicals, sugars, processed toxins, and old emotional baggage stored in the tissues.

As biohacking meets tradition, we now know that short fasts enhance autophagy (cellular renewal), boost stem cell production, balance hormones, and restore insulin sensitivity. The immune system gets a reset. The brain lights up. The mood lifts.

Guided juice cleanses can be paired with nature immersion and sauna, colon hydrotherapy, and lymphatic movement sessions to create a full-spectrum renewal experience. This is not just about what leaves the body but also about what reawakens.

Your fast can be three days, five days, seven, or more. Even a one-day reset each week can transform your chemistry. If you encounter resistance, detox symptoms, emotional releases, or fatigue – these are not signs of failure – they are signs of clearing, returning you to vitality.

Breath as a Blood Purifier

The lungs are often overlooked in the conversation around detoxification, yet every exhale you take is a release of waste. Carbon dioxide, cellular debris, volatile toxins – all are escorted out through the sacred rhythm of breath. Just as the bowels eliminate physical residue, lungs are gatekeepers of subtle purification. Unlike many bodily systems, this one is at our command. With every conscious breath, we hold the power to change our blood chemistry.

To exhale deeply, fully, with intention, is to wring the sponge of your cells. The purge of what no longer belongs is as important as the oxygen we take in. Stagnant breath leads to stagnant blood. Rhythmic, mindful breathing – especially with emphasized, forceful exhalations – helps regulate the nervous system, alkalize the body, release stored tension, and support lymphatic and emotional drainage. In many yogic and indigenous healing traditions, breath is revered as spirit, life force, *prana, ruach, qi*. Through breath we remember our aliveness.

Consider the coyote, when poisoned by bait left by trappers, will often run for miles, panting wildly – not in panic, but in instinctual purification. The panting is a purge. Through rapid respiration, the coyote moves toxins from the bloodstream before they reach critical organs. This is raw wisdom encoded in the body – an animal memory we share. We may not pant on all fours, but we can move our breath with the same urgency, same devotion to survival, same commitment to release.

Let this be your invitation: breathe like the Earth is cleansing you from the inside out. Let your inhale draw in life, and your exhale carry out pain, fear, stagnation, and residue. There is no cost, no ritual more accessible than this.

Step Four: Fueling the Body with Intelligence
Let Food Be Your Frequency

"The greatest tragedy that comes to man is emotional depression, the dulling of the intellect, and loss of initiative that comes from nutritive failure." — Dr. James McLester

What if your next meal was more than fuel? What if you ingested a transmission – a frequency capable of harmonizing your cells, uplifting your thoughts, and expanding your consciousness?

Step Four is about choosing food that is direct from Source – food that carries the sun's biophotons, earth's polyphenols, water's minerals, and universe's intelligence. We are not just what we eat. We become what our food has absorbed. The vibrational quality of that food is shaping our mental, emotional, and spiritual state.

In *The Way Knows*, we explored the idea that every molecule of food contains not just nutrients, but memory. Food is a cosmic messenger formed through the photosynthesis of starlight and grown through the geometry of sacred order. When we eat food with high vibrations – fresh, organic, raw, wild, and alive – we consume not just sustenance, but clarity.

Dr. David Hawkins, in his *Map of Consciousness*, revealed that everything has a measurable frequency. Processed food, fast food, and dead animal tissue vibrate at lower frequencies – matching the resonance of fear, guilt, and shame. Living, plant-based foods resonate higher – closer to love, joy, and peace.

This is not about diet. This is about light.

As we transition into fueling the body with intelligence, we will explore:

- Why Organic, Why Now
- Raw, Living Foods and Their Biophotons
- Understanding Plant-Based Nutrition
- Hidden Dangers in Processed Foods & GMOs
- Sugar, Gluten, and Inflammatory Culprits
- The Forgotten Power of Hydration

When we change the frequency of our food, we change the frequency of our thoughts. When we change the frequency of our thoughts, we become a tuning fork for joy.

Why Organic, Why Now

"We do not inherit the Earth from our ancestors; we borrow from our children." — Native Proverb

Organic food is a return to sanity, to harmony, to food that still remembers the sun. Eating clean is not a luxury. The word *"organic"* speaks to more than the absence of pesticides but also to the presence of life.

Organic crops grow in soils that are alive with beneficial microbes, fungi, and minerals. These microbes produce metabolites – plant medicines – that feed not only our bodies, but our cells' communication pathways, gut flora, and emotional resilience.

In a major review published in the *British Journal of Nutrition* (2014), researchers concluded that organic crops are up to sixty percent higher in a wide variety of health-promoting antioxidants than conventional crops. They also found significantly lower levels of cadmium – a toxic heavy metal – and a much lower presence of pesticide residues.

Eating organic food is not just about avoiding harm. This is about receiving more. More polyphenols. More minerals. More salicylic acid. More life force.

From the perspective of frequency, organic foods carry a different vibration. They have not been grown in depleted, lifeless soil. They are not sprayed with chemicals that disrupt endocrine function and kill off gut bacteria. Their biophotons – light particles absorbed from the sun – are still intact, ready to enliven our bodies.

As we learned in *The Way Knows*, real food is coded with intelligence. Cosmic rays, photon absorption, soil memory – all inform the food we consume. The more we attune to foods raised with care, reciprocity, and reverence, the more we reclaim this intelligence in our own tissues.

This is not a health trend. This is a return to communion between human and soil, consumer and earth. Choosing organic is not just self-care. This is planet care. Future care. A prayer for generations we will never meet.

Raw, Living Foods and Their Biophotons

"Keeping your body healthy is an expression of gratitude to the whole cosmos – the trees, the clouds, everything." — Thich Nhat Hanh

Raw, living foods are not just nutritional choices. They are light transmissions. They carry biophotons – tiny packets of solar energy – that communicate with our cells at the speed of light. This is food that is still vibrating with life.

Biophotons are quantum-level messengers encoded with frequency, memory, and information. When we eat raw, sun-fed fruits, vegetables, sprouts, and herbs, we are not just ingesting vitamins – we are absorbing pattern, order, and intelligence from the universe.

This is why the highest healing foods on the planet are not lab-made supplements, but the humble creations of sunlight and soil. Raw greens, wild berries, sea vegetables, fresh sprouts – all brimming with living structure and cosmic memory.

A study from the *International Journal of Food Sciences and Nutrition* (2009) noted that raw food diets are associated with significantly higher antioxidant status and lower body mass index. Another review in *Frontiers in Nutrition* (2022) emphasized the importance of enzyme-preserving foods for optimal digestive health and energy production.

Cooked food can nourish but living food regenerates. When we choose food that is still alive, our cells remember how to be alive. Our thoughts become sharper. Our skin begins to glow. Our connection to nature strengthens. Our cravings shift toward purity. This is not a diet but a reunion.

Allow the chlorophyll to return us to the forest. Let the minerals remind us of the mountains. May the enzymes teach us how to digest life more gently.

Understanding Plant-Based Nutrition

"Plants give us everything – light, structure, breath, and medicine. They are not just food. They are teachers." — Jesse J. Jacoby, *The Way Knows*

To understand plant-based nutrition is to understand nourishment at every level – cellular, emotional, ecological, and spiritual. A truly nourishing diet feeds and aligns the body. When we choose whole, unprocessed, organic plant foods, we align ourselves with the intelligence of nature.

We are not only avoiding what harms us (antibiotics, cholesterol, acidosis, inflammation); we are choosing what builds us, being fiber, antioxidants, enzymes, and phytochemicals that communicate directly with our genes and microbiome.

As detailed in *The Raw Cure 2.0*, the plant queendom offers everything the body needs to heal: minerals from deep earth soils, chlorophyll to oxygenate the blood, vitamin C to build collagen and immunity, and phytonutrients that protect the brain and nourish the heart. These elements are not just chemical; they are vibrational. They harmonize the biofield.

In *The High Life*, we explore how a clean plant-based diet dramatically improves biohacking outcomes – supporting detoxification, hormonal balance, gut integrity, and mental clarity. In a body free from meat, dairy, refined sugars, and chemicals, light flows more freely. The nervous system relaxes. Neurotransmitters stabilize. Spirit reinhabits the form.

You do not need to count macros or chase protein myths. The body thrives on color, texture, hydration, and variety. Plants provide complete amino acid profiles, abundant trace minerals, and prebiotic fibers that feed the microbiome – the root of emotional regulation and cognitive performance.

This is liberation, not a restriction. You have an opportunity to vote for life every time you fill your plate. Let your food be intelligent, emanating the rays from the sun, the rain, and the rhythm of seasons.

Hidden Dangers in Processed Foods & GMOs

"Anything that will not decompose in nature should never be placed in the body."

Processed foods, genetically modified organisms (GMOs), and synthetic additives may fill our shelves, but they deplete our bodies. These are not foods, they are facsimiles. Substitutes that hijack senses, dull the mind, and disrupt the gut-brain axis that governs our emotional resilience.

In *The High Life*, we examine the biochemical chaos caused by ultra-processed foods. GMOs, for example, are often laced with glyphosate – a potent herbicide linked to neuroinflammation, hormone disruption, microbiome destruction, and serotonin depletion. A 2013 study published in *Entropy* highlighted how glyphosate inhibits cytochrome P450 enzymes and disrupts gut flora, impacting mood and immune function at a systemic level.

Meanwhile, artificial dyes, emulsifiers, flavor enhancers, preservatives, and seed oils alter our neurochemistry and feed pathogenic microbes. These additives bypass our innate sensing system, the intuitive wisdom that once told us what to eat and what to avoid.

Processed foods often come fortified with synthetic vitamins and minerals, but they are devoid of life force. Their biophotons are gone. Their enzymes denatured. Their fiber stripped. What remains is a calorie-dense, nutrient-poor filler that clogs the body and fogs the mind.

What about GMOs? Their DNA has been edited for profit, not for nourishment. We consume crops whose design serves chemical resistance and corporate patents, not human vitality. To return to clarity, we must walk away from what is dead, manipulated, and artificial. We must remember what food really is: sunlight in edible form. Structure. Memory. Medicine.

Now we look more deeply into two major culprits that often hide in plain sight – sugar and gluten.

Sugar, Gluten, and Inflammatory Culprits

"Sugar offers comfort in the moment, but emptiness in the aftermath, feeding your cravings while starving your clarity."

Sugar and gluten are the twin seductions of modern nutrition – sweet and soft on the outside, inflammatory and insidious within. Refined sugar, in all forms – sucrose, high-fructose corn syrup, dextrose – hijacks dopamine pathways, depletes B vitamins and magnesium, feeds candida, and spikes insulin. Then, like a thief in the night, crashes mood, clarity, and resilience. Over time, these crashes build into depression, anxiety, and emotional fragility.

A 2022 study published in *Molecular Neurobiology* found that fructose consumption induces inflammation and oxidative stress, leading to alterations in mitochondrial function and changes in BDNF levels. These changes can negatively affect neuroplasticity and cognitive function, potentially contributing to mood disorders.

Additionally, a 2023 meta-analysis in *Frontiers in Nutrition* analyzed data from forty studies involving over 1.2 million participants. The analysis revealed that higher sugar intake was associated with a twenty-one percent increased risk of developing depression. The study suggests that consumption may influence depression risk through mechanisms involving BDNF levels and inflammation.

Gluten, meanwhile, is not the ancient grain of the past. Today's wheat is a hybridized, glyphosate-laced, high-gluten strain that disrupts gut permeability, triggers inflammation, and feeds pathogenic bacteria. Gluten's protein fractions – especially gliadin – stimulate zonulin, a compound that opens tight junctions in the gut lining. This leads to leaky gut and a cascade of neuroimmune responses that can mimic depression, fatigue, or brain fog.

In *The Way Knows*, we uncover how gut disruption equals spiritual disconnection. The more inflamed the body, the harder we struggle to hear the quiet voice of intuition.

Avoiding sugar and gluten is not about restriction but more about remembering how good feeling our best truly reverberates in our mood. This is about reclaiming the sovereignty of a clear mind and an open heart.

The Forgotten Power of Hydration

"Water is life's matter and matrix, mother and medium. There is no life without water." — Albert Szent-Györgyi

Hydration is more than a healthy tip; this is a sacred act of remembering. Water is the element of flow, language of life, and current that connects all living beings. Yet, in the modern world, we have forgotten how to drink wisely.

Every cell in the human body requires water to function. This is the solvent that carries nutrients, removes waste, cushions joints, regulates temperature, and enlivens our organs. Dehydration does not just dry the lips but also dulls cognition, stirs anxiety, slows detox, and can even contribute to depressive symptoms.

A 2018 study in *World Journal of Psychiatry* confirmed that insufficient hydration is linked to increased risk of depression and anxiety. Chronic low-grade dehydration inflames the body, compromises the blood-brain barrier, and stresses the adrenal system. Many people are walking around mildly dehydrated and emotionally off-balance without even knowing why.

The key is not just drinking more water but drinking the right water. Filtered. Mineralized. Structured. Distilled water, spring water, or filtered reverse osmosis water is ideal. Avoid chlorinated and fluoridated tap water. Stay away from water bottled in plastic. Re-mineralize your water with a pinch of red Alaea salt or a slice of cucumber.

We understand hydration as a bioelectrical event. A hydrated cell is a happy cell. Hydration allows us to receive more energy, channel more intuition, and metabolize life with more grace. Drink upon waking, between meals, and consistently throughout the day. Hydrate before you caffeinate.

Hydration is not only internal but is also reflected in our skin, eyes, and emotional expression. Well-hydrated skin appears soft, supple, and luminous – not because of expensive creams, but because the blood beneath flows freely and the tissues retain cellular elasticity. When we are dehydrated, the skin becomes dry, dull, and tight – mirroring constriction occurring within. The body knows when to conserve. Often, dehydration is not just from lack of water, but from oversaturation of acids – metabolic byproducts of stress, processed food, and emotional toxicity. In trying to buffer these acids, the body pulls water from our tissues, leading to dryness, stagnation, and premature aging.

One of the most overlooked sources of hydration is *living water* – the form of water found in raw fruits and vegetables, especially hydrating foods like watermelon, cucumber, oranges, and leafy greens. This water is often referred to as H_3O_2, or structured hydrogen water. Unlike plain H_2O, this form of water is more viscous, more coherent, and more bioavailable to the cells.

Water from sun-ripened produce enters the body along with fiber, enzymes, and minerals – providing not just hydration but electricity, magnetism, and vitality. Eating raw produce is one of the most efficient and harmonious ways to hydrate at a cellular level, aligning our internal terrain with the intelligence of nature.

Proper hydration is also emotional. The more hydrated you are, the more fluid your feelings are. You cry more easily. You digest emotion more freely. Water teaches us to move, to flow, to release. As the poet Rumi said, *"Try to be like the river that flows silently through the night, not fearing the darkness of the path."* This is the wisdom of water. Allow this substance to cleanse you, soften you, and become the quiet medicine that returns you to rhythm – both biological and cosmic.

Water, also, is not just for drinking. Think of cold plunges, saunas, and sweat. Herbal infusions. Water is therapy, a teacher, and a threshold. Let hydration be your ritual. Let your blood flow like spring rivers. Let your mind reflect the clarity of still water.

You are now prepared for Step Five – where you will reconnect with Earth, rewild your spirit, and begin to move your body in reverent motion.

Step Five: Reconnecting With Nature Through Movement

Embodiment is Medicine

"We are Earth walking. Breath wrapped in bones. And every step we take is a rhythm – an echo – calling us back to Source." —The Way Knows

In a world of mental overdrive and chronic disembodiment, Step Five calls us back into the body – toward sensation, presence, and Earth-contact. Here, we remember that healing is not just in the mind but in motion. In the muscle. In the land beneath our feet.

Somewhere along the way, we became heads atop screens – bodies forgotten, limbs underused, feet confined by concrete and soles. The body remembers the pulse of rivers, arc of trees, and spiraling wisdom of hips and spine. To return to nature is not only to walk the forest, but to feel yourself as a part of these vast ecosystems. Your bones carry the minerals of mountains. Your breath carries the rhythm of wind. Your blood mirrors the tide. Movement is the way the Earth speaks through you.

In Indigenous cultures across the globe, movement is never separated from meaning. A dance is a prayer. A walk is a ritual. Even a hunt is undertaken with reverence, each footfall part of a song passed down through generations. When we move with intention, our bodies become instruments of remembrance. Step Five invites us to move not to fix ourselves, but to feel ourselves. To return to a state of somatic reverence. To let each stretch, squat, breath, and step bring us back to a deeper intimacy with life.

This step is about communion through movement. We do not move just to burn calories; we move to awaken dormant energy. We move to harmonize with gravity. We move to remember we are not separate from Earth.

In this step, we explore:

- Grounding & Earth Resonance
- Intentional Exercise & Primal Mechanics
- Gardening and Soil Contact
- Walking Meditations & Outdoor Mindfulness
- The Sacred Science of Yoga

This is where healing becomes kinetic. Where we stop talking about transformation and begin to embody change.

Grounding & Earth Resonance

"To forget how to dig the earth and to tend the soil is to forget ourselves." — Mahatma Gandhi

Grounding, also known as Earthing, is the ancient and intuitive practice of touching Earth with bare skin. Beneath your feet lives a frequency and voltage – a subtle, healing hum of electrons and energy that your body recognizes and yearns for. Every time you step barefoot on soil, grass, or stone, your nervous system recalibrates.

Modern science now affirms what Indigenous wisdom has long known: when we connect with Earth's surface, we receive a bioelectrical reset. Studies show grounding reduces inflammation, normalizes cortisol, improves sleep, and balances serotonin. In the words of Dr. Tracy Latz of the Earthing Institute, *"Grounding stabilizes emotions, improving sleep architecture and decreasing the fight-or-flight response."*

Our ancestors walked barefoot, slept on the ground, and drank from springs. They were not *'grounding'* – they were simply living. The rise in inflammatory diseases, depression, and anxiety has paralleled our disconnection from this vital current.

In *The Way Knows*, we are reminded that the body is not just a machine but an antenna, and that Earth is the primary signal. There are stories among the Sami of Northern Europe about how hunters would sleep on moss beds to absorb the Earth's dreaming. Among Australian Aboriginal elders, walking barefoot across songlines – ancestral tracks embedded in the land – is not just travel, but a spiritual pilgrimage.

Try this yourself. Take off your shoes. Step onto the earth and feel what returns to you. Morning dew on the soles. Afternoon heat from sun-soaked stone. The evening coolness of the forest shadow. Let the planet teach you the rhythm of your own body.

Intentional Exercise & Primal Mechanics

"Movement is the song of the body." — Vanda Scaravelli

Our body is not designed to sit for hours beneath fluorescent lights. We were created to twist, leap, crouch, stretch, and spiral through space. In this age of artificial postures and sedentary routine, movement has become medicine – and when orchestrated well, a return to nature.

Functional patterns and primal mechanics offer us a way to remember how our bodies were meant to move. Not in isolated repetitions beneath metal machines, but through integrative, full-body motion that mimics our ancestors – walking, crawling, climbing, squatting, running.

At Soulspire, movement is rewilded. Through practices inspired by biomechanics, indigenous knowledge, and modern fascia science, we learn that the way we move shapes the way we feel. Movement is pattern reprogramming, not punishment. When we reset dysfunctional mechanics and train the body to move in harmony with gravity and breath, we free up pain, improve posture, and unlock mental clarity.

Modern studies confirm what elders have always known: rhythmic, grounded movement modulates cortisol, increases BDNF (brain-derived neurotrophic factor), and sharpens neuroplasticity. This combination boosts serotonin, enlivens digestion, and enhances proprioception.

From the Tarahumara runners of Mexico, whose barefoot endurance running rituals are woven into spiritual ceremony, to the Hadza tribes of Tanzania, whose daily hunting and foraging involves deep squats, long walks, and dynamic balance – primal motion is ancestral wisdom encoded in the body.

Start small. Relearn the squat. Practice crawling. Take your workouts to the forest. Instead of counting reps, count tree shadows, breath cycles, or the beat of birdsong. This is exercise as communion. This is movement as remembering.

Gardening and Soil Contact

"The garden is a process, not a place." — Jenny Uglow

To place your hands in soil is to press your palms into the skin of the Earth. In that contact lives an exchange far greater than calories or vitamins. There is remembrance, resonance, and renewal.

Gardening is more than growing food. This is ceremony, medicine, therapy. When we dig, we stir up not just roots and compost – but memories. Ancient ones.

Science now confirms what Indigenous wisdom has long known: there are microorganisms in healthy soil – such as *Mycobacterium vaccae* – that activate serotonin production in the brain, lifting mood, calming anxiety, and fortifying immune resilience. This is not folklore. This is biological reverence.

In *The Raw Cure 2.0*, we spoke about nature-deficit as one of the unspoken causes of despair. Gardening bridges that gap, placing our fingers back in dirt, breath back in rhythm with seasons, and minds back into creative flow.

To grow a plant from seed to harvest is to witness a slow miracle. In this slowness, there is medicine. We soften. We listen. We become part of something again. Every home should have a garden – even if only a pot of herbs on the windowsill.

Every child should know the feel of soil under their nails. Every neighborhood should reclaim unused lots and fill them with edible, flowering sanctuaries. Let your garden be a living prayer. Let your compost be alchemy. Let the soil remember who you are.

Walking Meditations & Outdoor Mindfulness

"Walk as if you are kissing the Earth with your feet." — Thich Nhat Hanh

Walking is one of the simplest and most powerful practices available to us. This requires no membership, no equipment, and no mastery. Yet when we walk with presence – mind in sync with breath, body in rhythm with land – we unlock a form of prayer that predates language.

Outdoor mindfulness is not about escaping life's challenges. We walk with them. We notice the way our thoughts shift as our feet press softly into dirt trails, sand, grass, or fallen leaves. We slow down enough to feel wind as medicine, birds as messengers, and shadows as teachers.

In *The Way Knows*, we speak of presence as a portal – and nowhere is this more accessible than on a mindful walk, through nature. This is not exercise but more of an attunement. A moving meditation.

Scientific research shows that mindful walking in green spaces lowers blood pressure, improves cognitive flexibility, and reduces cortisol levels more effectively than indoor movement. A 2020 study in *Frontiers in Psychology* revealed that mindful walking in nature increases connectedness, creativity, and emotional regulation.

There are stories told by Cherokee elders of walking before sunrise, feet on dewy grass, to receive guidance for the day. They called this *"receiving the whispers."* In Japanese tradition, shinrin-yoku – or *"forest bathing"* – is a form of healing in which one absorbs the forest atmosphere through the senses. Not thinking. Just being.

Try this: choose a trail or patch of green. Leave your headphones. Turn off your phone. Begin to walk slowly, barefoot if you can. With each step, repeat silently: *"Here."* With each breath, whisper inward: *"Now."* Let your pace be determined by your wonder.

The Sacred Science of Yoga

"Yoga is not about touching your toes but what you learn on the way down." — Jigar Gor

Yoga is the original technology of integration – teaching the nervous system to soften, mind to still, and breath to guide. This practice reunites our fragmented parts and makes the body a sanctuary for the soul.

Yoga is more than movement. Each posture is a mudra, each breath an offering, each sequence a ceremony. Through yoga, we recalibrate energy centers, stimulate the vagus nerve, and harmonize both hemispheres of the brain.

This is a science both mystic and measurable. Countless studies confirm that yoga reduces depression, balances cortisol, improves sleep, strengthens immunity, and increases GABA (gamma-aminobutyric acid) – a neurotransmitter responsible for calm and focus.

In ancient texts, yoga is defined not as posture, but as *union* – the yoking of the individual self with the cosmic whole. This is a return to coherence, remembering that we are never separate from Source. When the spine elongates, our breath deepens, and the gaze softens – we become conduits for sacred alignment. The mat becomes a mirror – reflecting our resistance, grace, effort, and surrender. What begins as movement becomes metaphor – for how we meet the world, hold discomfort, and return to center.

Indigenous traditions often speak of the body as a temple, not in metaphor, but in lived reverence. To enter the body through yoga is to walk the sacred halls of that temple. The pelvis becomes the hearth. The lungs – great chambers of wind. The hands – extensions of prayer. Whether your practice is ten minutes or two hours, elaborate or elemental, what matters is the intention: to inhabit yourself fully. To breathe as if the world is worth staying awake for. To move as if every joint is a hymn.

From the fire practices of Kundalini to the oceanic breath of Ujjayi in Vinyasa flow, yoga is a mirror of life: sometimes flowing, sometimes still, sometimes on fire. Always alive. Always sacred. Yoga is where movement becomes prayer. Where stillness becomes strength. Where we remember we are not just healing the body, we are awakening the being.

If you are new, begin gently. Start with sun salutations at dawn. Practice in your backyard. Light a candle and stretch in silence before bed. No performance or comparison is necessary. Just breath and presence. This is where the outer steps begin to reflect inner transformation. You are no longer just learning how to live. You are embodying transformation.

Step VI: Cultivating Substance

Feed Your Soul with Purpose

"True fulfillment comes not from accumulation, but from alignment – when what we do flows from who we are." — Jesse J. Jacoby, *The Way Knows*

Modern life often celebrates busyness, but neglects meaning. We are praised for performance yet starved of purpose. Step Six is a turning point that invites you to plant your roots deeper, step beyond survival, and begin to cultivate substance. This is where soul nourishment begins.

When we live with purpose – aligned with our unique gifts, driven by passion, and willing to grow – we shift from mere existence into creative embodiment. Substance is not what we possess but the quality of our presence. How we carry our talents, meet adversity, and shape the time we have been given.

Substance is not built overnight. Our composition is layered through ritual, reflection, and repeated acts of integrity. This forms when we rise after falling, we follow through on our values, and we offer something real to the moment we are in. In a culture that often rewards the surface, cultivating depth becomes a sacred rebellion.

In this step, we ask not how much we have achieved, but how much of ourselves we have brought into each experience. In the end, our resumes will not nourish us, our relationship to meaning will.

In this step, we explore:

- Discovering Talents and Joyful Expression
- Strengthening Character Through Challenge
- Lifelong Learning & Mental Expansion
- Creating Legacy Through Passion

Discovering Talents and Joyful Expression

"Life is painful, with thorns, like the stem of a rose. Culture and art are roses that bloom on the stem. The flower is your humanity. Art is the liberation of the humanity inside you." — Daisaku Ikeda

Each of us was born with a seed of brilliance. This might not look like fame or prestige, but pulses within us nonetheless – waiting for nourishment, for time, for our permission to grow. To discover your talents is an act of devotion, not ego. A way of honoring the gift of being alive.

Your talents may show up as art, song, kindness, leadership, craftsmanship, or humor. They may come in the form of attentive listening or fierce truth-telling. In many Indigenous cultures, talents were not *"chosen"* but revealed. Through rites of passage, dreams, or patterns seen by elders, your contribution was recognized and nurtured.

We live in a society that often asks what we do to earn a living, not what makes us feel alive. This step is about re-centering your joy. Let this force lead you. Explore. Play. Reclaim the hobbies left behind when life gets too serious.

Try something new: painting, dancing, climbing, sculpting, storytelling, singing in the forest, learning names of trees. Take a class. Ask your friends what they see as your gifts. Let curiosity pull you toward your forgotten pieces.

Always remember this: joyful expression is a healer. Studies show that engaging in creative pursuits lowers cortisol, increases dopamine, and improves neuroplasticity. Joy is part of the blueprint for your well-being. Whatever brings you into your heart – this is your compass.

As the Lakota elder Black Elk once said, *"The first peace, which is the most important, is that which comes within the souls of people when they realize their relationship, their oneness, with the universe."* Let joy reconnect you to that oneness.

Strengthening Character Through Challenge

"Be more concerned with your character than reputation, because character is what you really are, while reputation is merely what others think you are." — John Wooden

Character is forged in the fire of experience, shaped by how we rise when we fall, how we choose when no one is watching, and how we treat those who cannot repay us.

In many Indigenous teachings, character is taught through story, silence, and service, not through rules. A young person learns integrity by how they tend the fire for elders, how they walk through the forest, and how they carry themselves in the unseen. Character is energy you bring into the room, not performance, but presence.

In a world obsessed with image, Step Six invites us to return to essence. To live in alignment with the Six Pillars of Character: Trustworthiness, Respect, Responsibility, Fairness, Caring, and Citizenship. These are vibrations, not just virtues. When we embody them, our lives become medicine for others.

Challenge is a forge for refinement, not something to avoid. From heartbreak to hardship, every trial offers an invitation to grow more rooted, more real. Just as the acacia tree in the Kalahari bends under drought to survive, so too can we adapt, deepen, and become more alive through difficulty and duress.

The goal is authenticity, not perfection. To be someone who lives in harmony with their values, even when the world pulls them elsewhere. Do hard things. Show up for what matters. Speak truth, even when your voice trembles. That is how character grows.

Let's continue to expand the mind, where your inner fire is fed by new knowledge.

Lifelong Learning & Mental Expansion

"A good head and a good heart are always a formidable combination. But when you add to that a literate tongue or pen, then you have something very special." — Nelson Mandela

Learning is not confined to classrooms. This is the river that feeds our roots long after formal schooling ends. To engage the mind in new knowledge is to declare: *I am still alive, still becoming, still curious.*

Whether through reading, researching, or observing the natural world, expanding your mind is an act of defiance against stagnation. A sacred celebration of the brain's plasticity – the ability to grow new neural pathways, forge fresh insight, and awaken dormant memory.

In many Indigenous communities, wisdom is not measured by certificates but by how well one listens to the land, the elders, and the voice inside which whispers, *"keep going."* The great oral traditions of our ancestors were built upon story, silence, and seasonal learning.

In today's world, we have the great gift of access. Free courses from institutions around the globe are offered on platforms like Coursera and TEDx. Languages await Duolingo. Thousands of books rest on shelves or inside devices, waiting to rewire the heart.

Research shows that those who pursue lifelong learning reduce their risk of cognitive decline, increase adaptability, and enhance emotional intelligence. Learning a new skill, like playing an instrument or studying a language, stimulates the hippocampus and slows age-related memory loss.

You do not need to know where this leads. Just begin. Pick up a book. Listen to a podcast on the medicine of mushrooms. Take a course in Indigenous permaculture. Learn the stars by name. Learning is nourishment.

Creating Legacy Through Passion

"Many people die with their music still in them. Why is this so? Too often because they are always getting ready to live. Before they realize, time runs out." — Oliver Wendell Holmes

Legacy is not something we leave behind. This is the ripple of our choices, our presence, our creations. How the Earth remembers us when our name has faded.

To live with passion is to live with fire – not a fire that burns wildly, but one that warms, illuminates, and cooks something meaningful. What you do with your days becomes the mosaic of your years. What you love, when lived boldly, becomes your gift to the world.

We have been conditioned to believe that legacy comes from status or wealth, but real legacy is written in love. In the impact we have on those we meet. In how we speak to strangers. In how we touch the land. In what we choose to make with our time.

The elders of many Indigenous lineages speak of walking *"with seven generations in mind."* That your every action echoes through the lives of those not yet born. When you plant a tree, teach a song, save a stream, or love deeply – you are creating memory in the web of life.

Maybe your legacy is art. Maybe mentoring. Maybe a community garden, a song you will sing into the winds, or a ritual your children will remember. The form does not matter. The intention does.

If you have not started yet, start now. There is no retirement for the soul. Your spirit is still listening to the sound of your own song.

Let passion be the compass.

Let your legacy be love made visible.

Step Seven: Purifying Your Sphere of Influence

Audit Your Environment

"You are the average of the five people you spend the most time with." — Jim Rohn

Our environment shapes us more than we realize. Like rivers carving canyons, the energies and attitudes of those around us leave lasting impressions on the terrain of our spirit. Step Seven invites us to become conscious curators of our connections. To choose wisely. To protect the garden of our becoming.

We often underestimate subtle ways energy moves between people. A sigh, a glance, a complaint left unchecked – these small exchanges either nourish our nervous system or drain us. Just as we are mindful of the food we consume; we must also become mindful of the emotional and energetic *"diet"* we take in through our relationships. The people we allow close to our heart shape our internal weather. Are they storm clouds or sunlight? Fertile soil or chronic drought?

This is not about judgment or superiority but about resonance. As we evolve, some connections will fall away naturally, like old leaves releasing in autumn. Others will deepen, anchoring us into truth and mutual growth. Step Seven is about releasing obligation and stepping into alignment. We are creating an ecosystem of support, integrity, and inspiration. The more intentional our circle becomes, the clearer we hear the voice of our soul.

In this step, we explore:

- Conscious Awareness of Influence
- Relationships That Elevate
- Redefining Success From the Inside Out

Conscious Awareness of Influence

"Keep away from people who try to belittle your ambitions. Small people always do that, but the great ones make you feel that you too can become great." — Mark Twain

Every soul we invite into our space leaves an imprint. Some plant joy. Some carry shadows. To walk the path of healing, we must become discerning gardeners of relationships. In the words of Indigenous elders, *"You must know who walks beside you in the dark, not just in daylight."*

Guilt by association is not only a legal phrase but is also an energetic truth. When we tether ourselves to people steeped in bitterness, fear, or dysfunction, we absorb what they carry. This is ecology, not judgment. Your spirit is sacred terrain. You must be vigilant of what you allow to take root.

Some influences are loud – criticism, manipulation, and drama. Others are subtle – apathy, avoidance, or energetic dissonance that leaves you drained without knowing why. Pay attention to how you feel after time with someone. Do you feel uplifted or unsettled? Clear or confused? Inspired or contracted? These signals are sacred data. Your body and intuition are speaking – tune in.

As we grow in consciousness, our resonance shifts. We begin to crave depth over distraction, honesty over convenience, and relationships that water our roots. This does not mean we only surround ourselves with perfection; this means we magnify our presence. With people who are also doing the work. People who reflect, not deflect. People who help you remember who you are when you forget.

As you awaken, you may find your path diverging from old companions. This is growth, not betrayal. When you lead with love, sometimes even those you left behind find their way to your light.

Relationships That Elevate

"Anybody can be unhappy. We can all be hurt. We must be concerned about other people, regardless." — Willie Nelson

The company we keep becomes the climate we live in. Just as plants thrive in specific soil, we too need a nourishing social ecosystem. Surround yourself with people who remind you of your light. Whose eyes mirror joy. Those who challenge you with love, not judgment. The ones who listen with their whole presence and cheer you on when you rise.

Positive relationships are medicine. They regulate your nervous system. They rewire your emotional patterns. They teach your body what safety and celebration feel like.

If someone consistently drains you, belittles your purpose, or muddies your clarity – they may not belong in your front row. This does not mean casting them out in anger but protecting your peace with reverence.

Elevated relationships do not require perfection – they oblige presence. The people who elevate you are often those who have walked through their own fire and still choose softness. They hold space without needing to fix you. They reflect your potential even when you forget. In their presence, you feel seen, not managed. Supported, not steered. These are the ones to hold close – those who feed your soul's expansion without ever demanding you shrink to fit their version of love.

In Indigenous cultures, relationships are not transactional. They are ceremonial. Each interaction is a chance to give gratitude, offer presence, and build reciprocal energy. Allow your relationships to be reflections of the person you are becoming. Be the kind of person someone would write a poem about. Build a circle that brings out your sacredness.

Redefining Success from the Inside Out

"Wealth is love, music, sports, learning, family and freedom. Remember that every day contains a universe of potential."

Success is the depth of your presence, not the sum of your possessions. How your life impacts the lives of others. Whether you are remembered with warmth or with absence. In Step Seven, we redefine the meaning of success, not by the weight of your wallet, but the depth of your wisdom. Not by followers, but by footprints left on hearts.

Who you spend time with reflects what you believe about yourself. Are you surrounded by inspiration or obligation? Do your closest people pull you forward or anchor you in fear? Make a list of those who influence you most. Count integrity, vision, laughter, courage, and soul.

Redefining success means shedding the inherited scripts of achievement and tuning into the quiet knowing of the soul. True success is when you can look at your life and say: *I am living in alignment. My days reflect my values. My energy feeds what matters.*

Embodiment is waking up with peace in your chest and going to sleep without regret. In many Indigenous traditions, success is measured not by what you accumulate, but by how generously you give, how deeply you listen, and how well you remember your place in the great web of life.

In this new paradigm, success looks like emotional fluency. Like a body cared for with reverence. Like a home filled with plants, books, and people who reflect your appearance. You flourishing is having the courage to say no to the superficial so you can say yes to what is sacred. When you redefine success from the inside out, you become immune to hollow applause. Your fulfillment becomes your own applause – that which echoes forever.

Step Eight: Releasing Expectations

Dismantle the Invisible Prison

"There is no gate, no lock, no bolt that you can set upon the freedom of my mind." — Virginia Woolf

Step Eight invites us to loosen the tight threads of performance, comparison, and inherited obligation. We pause here; to take inventory of the silent contracts we have signed with the world – agreements to be what others expect – and we begin to rewrite them in our own language.

Expectations are often inherited like family heirlooms –handed down unconsciously, yet heavy with meaning. We carry the dreams our parents never lived, the fears our culture clings to, the stories our lineage repeats. In this step, we begin to hand those burdens back – not with bitterness, but with reverence. We thank them for what they tried to offer, and then we release them. We cannot walk our truest path wearing someone else's shoes.

To release expectations is to reclaim authorship of your life, and ask, *what is mine to carry?* To sit with the question, *who am I when no one is watching?* Here we learn that peace does not come from doing what is expected, but from doing what is aligned. We remember that joy requires presence, not permission.

To live without expectations is not to live without vision but without the weight of someone else's dream. Let's begin by opening the door to the invisible prison and walking out.

In this step, we explore:

- Freeing the Mind from Mental Constructs
- Detaching From Comparison
- Honoring Your Unique Path

Freeing the Mind from Mental Constructs

"We are raised on comparison. Our education and culture are based on correlation, so, we struggle to be someone other than who we are." — Jiddu Krishnamurti

Expectations can act as invisible walls – these structures we did not build but find ourselves trapped within. We inherit blueprints: from family, society, school, religion. Be this. Do that. Make money. Look good. Stay safe. The soul was not born to be confined.

In many Indigenous traditions, children were not raised to be molded, but to be revealed. Elders would observe a young person's behavior, dreams, voice, and energy to discern their gifts. The role of community was not to impose identity but to witness into form.

Mental constructs are not only inherited, but they are also reinforced by repetition. The more often we tell ourselves a story, even if false, the more we shape this into reality. *"I am not enough." "I should be further along." "I cannot disappoint them."* These inner scripts shape the limits of our becoming. Beliefs are not truths, they are agreements. The powerful truth is this: *we can choose to stop agreeing.*

Freedom begins the moment we question the voices we have mistaken for our own. You are directed to rewrite the narrative, to speak to yourself with the gentleness no one ever modeled for you. The mind, once conditioned to obey old masters, may resist. You are not the programming they indoctrinated you with. You are the consciousness behind all – wild, worthy, and free.

To free ourselves from mental slavery, as Bob Marley reminded us, *we must first become conscious of the chains.* Are you living someone else's dream? Are your goals born from love or from pressure? Prison is made of beliefs, not bricks. Let this step be your jailbreak.

Detaching From Comparison

"A river never compares herself to the ocean. She flows in her own direction, carrying life just the same." — The Way Knows

Comparison invites us into a competition no one wins – severing us from our wholeness and setting our gaze on illusions. Social media has become a stage of curated perfection. Behind every highlight reel is a human – flawed, sacred, longing, just like you.

You are not here to be like them. You are here to be like you. When we compare, we forget that each soul has a distinct curriculum. Some grow quickly; others ripen with time. Both oaks and wildflowers belong. There is no hierarchy in authenticity.

The Indigenous Quechua people of the Andes remind us that every element of nature plays a role in the song of life. The condor does not compare to the hummingbirds, they simply fly in their own sky.

Comparison drains our creativity and distracts us from the sacred work of becoming. When we measure our worth against someone else's journey, we silence the original song we were born to sing. Just as no two seeds bloom in the same season, no two lives unfold in the same rhythm. Some of our most profound growth happens underground, in unseen soil.

In many ancestral teachings, the concept of *"enough"* is sacred. You are not meant to be more like them. You are meant to be more like yourself. When we let go of comparison, we return to presence. We remember that life is a ritual, not a race. Your very existence, when you live in alignment, is an offering to the world.

Honor your timeline. Celebrate your cadence.

Honoring Your Unique Path

"To be beautiful means to be yourself. You do not need to be accepted by others, you need to accept yourself." — Thich Nhat Hanh

You came here with a reason. With some recipe for your own medicine. A message. Your job is not to meet others' expectations but to remember who you are and live fully. We are each born with a path that is carved not by maps but by footsteps. You will not find yours by copying someone else's. You discover your dharma by walking into what lights you up. By listening to what breaks your heart and moves your spirit.

Whether your path is humble or grand or unfolds in the wild or within the quiet corners of a village – walk in the direction of your mission with your whole being. In the sacred Lakota language, the phrase *Mitákuye Oyás'iŋ* means *"all my relations."* This reminds us that each life is interwoven with the whole. When you honor your core values, you serve the circle.

There is no template for your becoming. Just as no two trees bend the same in the wind, no two souls bloom in identical patterns. Your timing, your trials, your gifts – they are part of an ancient design coded uniquely within you. To honor your path is to stop apologizing for your pace. To trust that even when the way is unclear, your inner compass knows the terrain. The path unfolds not through force, but through faithful presence. Keep walking. Your life is not behind you but is becoming you.

Let go of who you were taught to be. Live the life your soul remembers. We are now ready for Step Nine, where compassion extends beyond the self and begins to radiate outward, shaping a more unified world.

Step Nine: Expanding Consciousness

Awaken Your Inner Light

"The real voyage of discovery consists not in seeking new landscapes, but in having new eyes." — Marcel Proust

At the crest of our healing journey, as we begin to reassemble the luminous mosaic of our soul, we are invited into the ninth step: an awakening of consciousness. This step is not about arriving at certainty but about deepening our sensitivity to life. Here, the aperture of perception widens. Here, we remember our place not as separate beings in a random universe, but as threads woven through the living fabric of Earth and all her relations.

This is where the mind softens into the heart and the veil of separation begins to dissolve. The idea of *"me"* and *"them," "us"* and *"nature,"* slowly disintegrates in the warmth of radical empathy. As indigenous elders have taught for millennia, we are born from, not into the world. We are not visitors here, but kin among kin.

To expand consciousness is not to reach toward the heavens and escape this earthly plane but to go deeper into the soil of our being, to tend to the roots of what makes us human. This kind of awakening does not happen all at once. We experience an unfolding. A listening to the soul-song that sings beneath the static. We begin to remember.

In the words of the Kogi people of the Sierra Nevada mountains, who refer to themselves as the *"Elder Brothers"* and the rest of modern humanity as the *"Younger Brothers,"* the *Earth is not ours to conquer, but to care for.* We do so best when we see through the eyes of unity, and when we feel the heartbeat of the planet pulse through our own chests. This is the pulse of expanded awareness, the drumbeat of collective healing.

Radical Compassion & Reverence for Life

"When you feel the suffering of every living thing in your own heart, that is consciousness." — Bhagavad Gita

To be conscious is not merely to think more or to collect spiritual jargon. We see with clarity the way our choices reverberate through the web of life. Indigenous elders have always taught that the Earth is a sentient being and every act of harm we commit, whether to the soil, animals, or one another, reflects a wound within our own psyche. As we begin to feel again – deeply, wholly – we cannot help but be moved to compassion.

This is radical compassion: the kind that does not flinch from sorrow but is embraced; that knows a trembling deer has a song of wisdom as valid as any sacred text; that sees a homeless man as no less divine than a king. Our reverence must extend not only to what is beautiful and easy to love, but to what is uncomfortable, inconvenient, and even painful to behold.

As Richard Rudd writes in the *Gene Keys*, *"True compassion emerges when we see with the eyes of unity rather than division."* To live compassionately in an unconscious world is no easy feat. We are asked to be bridgebuilders between worlds – the seen and unseen, the convenient and the right. In doing so, we elevate our own vibrational field and help restore the memory of harmony within the human story.

Radical compassion is participatory. We are asked to feel and to act from that feeling. This is demonstrated in how we speak to a child, how we vote with our fork and dollar, and how we show up. In the words of Martín Prechtel, *"You cannot know the sacred unless you bleed for your convictions."* Compassion is a sacred vow to protect what is vulnerable, to honor what is overlooked, and to walk through the world with tenderness as our strongest armor.

Practicing True Forgiveness

"Forgiveness is the fragrance that the violet sheds on the heel that has crushed her." — Mark Twain

Forgiveness is the alchemy of the heart. The sacred fire that transmutes resentment into wisdom. In this stage, we do not pretend that harm has not been done, but we choose to free ourselves from all bondage. As indigenous healers often say, *"When you do not forgive, the poison stays in you."*

To forgive is not to condone but to reclaim our power. We release ourselves from the entanglement of another's unconsciousness. Whether we are forgiving a parent who did their best with limited tools, a friend who betrayed us, or a system that has failed the people, we are cutting cords and restoring our sovereignty.

True forgiveness begins with us. We must offer mercy to our past versions who were blind, afraid, or simply lost. When we forgive ourselves, we release the shame that clouds our light, and we remember that healing is not perfection, but integration.

Forgiveness is an act of ceremony that when not forced, arrives like rainfall after drought – as the ground is ready to receive. Sometimes the entrance is quiet, like a softening in the chest. Other times, with grief and trembling. Whichever the path of emergence, this expression brings relief, like a burden set down after being carried too far.

The Haudenosaunee speak of the Great Law of Peace, in which reconciliation is woven into the governance of the people. Forgiveness, they teach, is what allows the circle to remain unbroken. To forgive in a culture that rewards vengeance is an act of rebellion. To release others from the debt of our pain is to become free in ways that punishment never offers. When we forgive, we do not forget – we reweave. We compost the old story into medicine.

Grace for Human Mistakes

"An error does not become a mistake until repeated."

To elevate our consciousness is not to rise above the mess of human life, but to find grace within. Mistakes are the soil of transformation. They show us where our love must grow roots. We are all stumbling toward wholeness, each of us guided by the mysterious hand of life.

From a shamanic perspective, a mistake is often the soul's detour to deepen our medicine. This is not a failure, but a necessary descent into the underworld to retrieve lost power. What matters most is not that we get everything right, but that we remain teachable.

When we allow ourselves and others to be human – flawed, contradictory, evolving – we invite a culture of authenticity. We no longer fear failure, because we understand that the compost of our errors feeds the garden of our awakening.

To offer grace is to hold space for unfolding – knowing wisdom does not descend fully formed but is shaped in the slow curve of becoming. In the teachings of many Indigenous cultures, mistakes are not sins to be punished but teachers to be honored. The misstep is not the end but is often the exact point where the path begins to turn sacred. As Martín Prechtel writes, *"To become a real human being, one must enter the broken places and plant beauty there."*

We are not meant to walk through life without bruises. We are meant to gather meaning from the impact. Grace does not excuse harm but does remind us that we are more than our worst moment. That every time we choose to repair, to apologize, to grow, we mend the invisible threads that connect us to the whole. In this way, grace becomes a living practice, a soft fire we keep lit, for ourselves and for each other, especially when the night feels long.

Acceptance of the Journey

"The cure for the pain is in the pain." — Rumi

There comes a moment when we start dancing with difficulty, rather than attempting to escape. This is the grace of acceptance. When we no longer fight the current, we learn how to flow. The sacred traditions of the Andes speak of *Ayni* – sacred reciprocity. Life is always in motion, always in exchange. When we surrender to this rhythm, we find our place within the pulse of the cosmos.

Acceptance means recognizing that everything, even pain, has a purpose. We honor the crooked path as holy. We trust the unfolding even when we do not yet understand the shape. As we embrace this step, our consciousness expands not just upward, but outward and inward. We become vessels for compassion, forgiveness, humility, and peace. In doing so, we embody the true nature of awakening: not as an escape from the world, but as a deeper participation.

Acceptance allows us to lay down the burden of resistance and begin to gather the wisdom that only experience can offer. In the Lakota way, the sacred hoop of life is not about arrival but inclusion. Every joy and sorrow, every gain and loss, belongs. When we stop pushing away parts of the journey, we begin to walk in wholeness. We no longer brace for life; we bow in reverence.

In the next step, we will explore how the cultivation of service completes the circle and allows us to become living medicine for a world in need.

Step Ten: Trusting the Orchestration

Everything Has Meaning

"When we try to isolate anything, we find threads hitched to everything else in the Universe." — John Muir

There is a mysterious symmetry woven into the fabric of our lives – an invisible choreography that guides us through joy and grief, contraction and expansion, birth and death. In this Tenth Step, we are invited to surrender to the truth that we are not random wanderers through a chaotic universe, but participants in a divine unfolding.

This step is the sacred pause where we look back, not with regret, but with reverence. The turning point where pain becomes teacher, and wounds become oracles. *"Why is this happening to me?"* becomes *"What is this trying to show me?"* In that simple shift, consciousness ripens.

Among the Andean people, there is a word: *ayni* – sacred reciprocity – which describes the cosmic balance of give and receive, of action and consequence, of grief and grace. When we live in alignment with *ayni*, we begin to see that every detour is part of a map we do not yet understand. When heartbreaks arrive or plans fall apart, this is redirection, not punishment. This is life's intelligence reorienting us to something more whole.

The Lakota speak of *Wakan Tanka*, the Great Mystery. To them, what appears as chaos is the movement of the sacred. What we call coincidence; they may call guidance. Every meeting, every delay, every loss may hold an encoded medicine for our becoming. Life is a spiral, not a straight line. We revisit wounds not because we are broken, but because we are deepening. Circling closer to the truth. In trusting the orchestration, we release the illusion that we are supposed to be anywhere else than where we are.

Plotkin reminds us that soul is not a goal to achieve but a mystery to embody. Our detours may be the holy roads leading us home. To trust the orchestration of life is to remember that there are no wasted experiences. Even the most bewildering moments, the ones that fracture us, contain hidden strands of gold.

The ancient Taoists believed that the universe organizes according to an elegant, invisible order – the Way, or *Dao* – which cannot be grasped with the intellect but can be sensed through surrender. When we cease resisting and soften into the flow, the orchestration becomes audible. Like hearing a distant flute in the forest, subtle but unmistakable.

In the Quechua language, there is no word for *"despair."* The worldview holds that all things are interrelated and purposeful – even the dark nights. Suffering is seen not as punishment but as a teacher, a sacred ally sent to initiate transformation. When we honor life's orchestration with ceremony and reverence, we discover meaning in the mess and beauty in the breakdown. This is an example of embodied trust born of experience.

When we begin to trust that we are already being guided, our nervous systems soften. Life becomes less about striving and more about sensing. We stop pushing against the tide and begin to move with her rhythm.

This is where synchronicity becomes language, where mystery becomes mentor. When we see our journey through this lens, even the sharpest moments of pain are reframed – not as wrong turns, but as sacred instructions from a wiser, more ancient rhythm within.

Finding Purpose in Pain

"Hardships prepare ordinary people for an extraordinary destiny." — C.S. Lewis

Every soul on the path of awakening is eventually brought to their knees. The loss of a job, the death of a loved one, a betrayal, a health crisis, the unraveling of identity – these moments feel like ruin, but in truth, they are thresholds. They initiate us into a deeper intimacy with life. In this crucible, a new self begins to take shape.

As mythologist Michael Meade says, *"Where there is wound, there is myth."* Pain is the invitation from, not polarity of healing. Many indigenous rites of passage begin in ordeal because the elders know that true wisdom does not come cheap and is earned through fire. Some of the most intricate insight is whispered in darkness and retrieved in solitude.

Manly P. Hall once wrote, *"When the human soul suffers enough, he begins to ask the right questions."* Those questions birth reverence, which leads to compassion, and finally to conception of a new world.

In Q'ero tradition of the high Andes, illness is not seen as punishment, but as a message from Pachamama (Mother Earth) calling the soul back into alignment. Pain is the system's way of rebalancing what has been forgotten, not a flaw. We are invited to listen, sit in the fire, and hear what the wound is asking of us. Pain, when honored, becomes a passage to sacred purpose.

The San Bushmen of the Kalahari say that when a person falls ill, the soul is calling for a song to be sung back into the body. They do not ask what is wrong, they ask: *when did you stop dancing? When did you stop singing? When did you stop listening to the stories of the ancestors?* Pain is not only an indicator of imbalance but is an echo of a deeper song waiting to be remembered.

Like seeds cracking open underground, our pain can be the pressure that births new life. It forces us inward, toward the dark soil of introspection, and from there, our roots can find water. Our hearts, broken open, become chalices for deeper wisdom to pour in. In the lineage of wisdom keepers, it is often said: the wound is the womb. That which breaks us can also birth us.

From Breakdown to Breakthrough

"All great changes are preceded by chaos." — Deepak Chopra

Breakdowns are not the end of the road; they are the compost of awakening. Just as forests regenerate through fire, our inner landscape often must be cleared of false constructs, limiting beliefs, and outdated stories. What feels like falling apart is often the soul's way of saying: *you are ready for more.*

In Dagara tradition of West Africa, crisis is seen as a sacred messenger. Malidoma Somé taught that illness, depression, and misfortune often signal that a soul is being summoned to remember a purpose. When the old ways no longer fit, the soul shouts. Breakdown is not pathology; this is a rite of renewal.

We can learn to honor these seasons. To grieve without shame. To break without fearing that we are broken. In the words of Richard Rudd, *"When you truly trust the path, even your missteps are sacred."*

Each breakdown holds within, the seed of breakthrough. Each dark night bears a promise of dawn. Just as the caterpillar disintegrates before becoming a butterfly, so too must we surrender to the mystery of becoming. The cocoon is not the end but is the sacred in-between.

The Pueblo peoples tell stories of how humanity was born from the womb of the Earth – through cycles of emergence from darkness into light. They believe that our soul evolves in stages, and each collapse is an invitation to step into a new world, more aware, more whole. The breakdown is not a curse but a sacred summons.

In the Celtic lore of Brigid, the goddess of poetry and fire, we are reminded that before the forge can shape metal, the material must be melted down. So too, our souls must sometimes be softened by the fire of adversity before we are ready to carry our truest form. In this way, breakdown becomes the holy forge of transformation.

Among the Inuit, there is a belief that the cracks in the ice are where the light enters. In our lives, those cracks – our breakdowns – are not signs of weakness, but of readiness. When something deep within us can no longer hold the weight of untruth, illusion, or suppression, this begins to split – not to destroy us, but to let something more honest emerge. This is how the soul reclaims the body. This is how truth channels back into the heart. Let yourself crack open, not in despair, but in devotion to what you want to have.

Everything Has Meaning

"In every loss, there is a hidden seed. In every ending, the whisper of a beginning."
— Robin Wall Kimmerer

To trust the orchestration of life is to meet suffering with the eyes of a deeper knowing. Nothing is wasted. Not a tear. Not heartbreak. Not even the years we thought were lost. Everything is being used, metabolized, alchemized into the raw material of awakening.

Here in the Tenth Step, we are asked to relinquish control and embrace surrender – not as weakness, but as sacred strength.

We become available to miracles not because we manipulate the timeline, but because we attune to the rhythm beneath the noise. We let go of needing all the answers, and in letting go, we begin to hear the music. This is not the end. This is the invitation to begin again, with clearer eyes and a fuller heart. Trust the orchestration. Trust the chaos. Trust the call.

In Celtic tradition, life is viewed as a spiral path, not a linear one. Each twist and turn brings us deeper into the center of our being. When we embrace this cyclical wisdom, we stop resisting the fall. We begin to see that even the collapse carries us closer to the soul's radiance.

Rumi once said, *"Try not to resist the changes that come your way. Instead, let life live through you."* In trusting the orchestration, we let life breathe through us. We become instruments of the music, and realize what a mysterious, wondrous symphony this really is.

The Hopi elders speak of the river that is moving fast. They say to let go of the shore, push off into the current, and keep our heads above water. This is the time of the lone wolf no longer. Look around and see who is in the water with you. Celebrate the journey, knowing that the current is wise. Trust that it knows the way home.

Trusting in orchestration is to walk in the dark with open palms – knowing that what you hold may not be what you expected but will always be what you needed for the next chapter of your unfolding. You are not lost; you are being woven.

In Step Eleven, we will gather all we have remembered and start crafting a new vision – one rooted in purpose, one aligned with joy, one that allows our healed selves to be of service to the world.

Step Eleven: Building a Vision & Action Plan

Manifest Your New Life

"The soul does not dream simply to escape life but to reveal how life could become more whole." — Bill Plotkin

There comes a moment on every sacred journey when the pilgrim turns, not to look behind. but ahead. In Step Eleven, we do this. We turn toward the horizon, not as a lost wanderer, but as one who remembers. One who now walks with their ancestors at their back and the future in their palm. This is the sacred architecture of manifestation. The drawing down of dreams into form, the weaving of soul truths into tangible action. What was once fragmented is now forged into clarity.

The poet David Whyte calls this the act of *"shaping a life as if a work of art."* What else could your healing be but a masterpiece in progress? Through ten sacred steps, we have shed skin, unearthed roots, cried prayers into the dirt, and stretched our arms toward the sun. Now, in this Eleventh Step, we give shape to the emergent self. We make a map – not of escape, but of return. A homecoming to purpose.

In many Indigenous traditions, vision is not something we chase but something we receive. The Lakota *hanbleceya*, the vision quest, is undertaken not to find an ambition, but to be found by the Great Mystery. In this step, we do not force a plan—we listen for one. The plan is already inscribed in your being. Your job now is to tune in and respond.

Bill Plotkin reminds us that soul initiation is never merely a moment of clarity but is a transition into sacred responsibility. To know is not enough. To act is the demand of the soul. Manly Hall echoes this when he writes, *"All men who have the power to act are under divine obligation to act."* Your healing, therefore, is not just yours. This is the seed of collective renewal.

So, we gather the threads. We revisit each truth, each shedding, each step. We begin to craft the altar of our new life: step by step, intention by intention, breath by breath. What you imagine now, you make sacred through action. The bridge between dreaming and doing is made of will, of grace, and of rhythm.

Reviewing the Foundation

"To forget one's ancestors is to be a brook without a source, a tree without root." — Chinese Proverb

Before any structure rises, the ground must be blessed. The land must be cleared, honored, and understood. So too, we begin Step Eleven by reviewing the sacred terrain we walked. These ten steps were not just ideas, they were rituals. They asked for your sweat, your tears, your courage. Now, they offer you a firm foundation.

Step One revealed the culprits, the roots of our despair, both internal and systemic. We named the shadows. In Step Two, we reclaimed our perception and the alchemy of attitude. In Step Three, we opened the inner gates of cleansing, letting go of toxicity not only from food but from memory, emotion, and stagnation. Step Four nourished us with vibrant fuel, teaching us that food is frequency, and that the Earth wants to feed our joy.

In Step Five, we returned to the primal rhythm of movement, touching soil, breath, and body as sacred instruments. Step Six asked us to cultivate substance, to remember that we are not our resumes or our roles – but our relationships, our curiosities, our art. In Step Seven, we purified our sphere of influence. We chose resonance over proximity, surrounding ourselves with those who breathe life into our vision.

By Step Eight, we released the invisible prison of expectations. We stopped contorting our lives into someone else's blueprint. In Step Nine, we expanded our consciousness. We learned to think like a forest, feel like a river, and love like a mountain – rooted, wide, and full of sky. Step Ten asked us to surrender to orchestration – to trust that even our tears have sacred timing.

Now, with these ten stones in our medicine pouch, we are ready to build. Not out of desperation, but out of devotion. Your foundation is not what you have survived, but what you have remembered. You are not beginning again; you are starting forward.

Setting Empowered Intentions

"You are what your deepest desire is. As your desire is, so is your intention. As your intention is, so is your will. As your will is, so is your deed. As your deed is, so is your destiny." — Brihadaranyaka Upanishad

Intention is not a wish but a vow. A commitment made in the chambers of your heart and sealed in the drumbeat of your actions. In the Indigenous traditions of the Yawanawá people of the Amazon, intention is often spoken before ayahuasca ceremonies as a compass for the spirit. They believe that what you call in with clarity, Spirit will amplify.

We begin here by defining the life you are now choosing. Not vaguely, not someday, but with boldness and precision. *What does your ideal day look like? What nourishes your body, your spirit, your mind? Who surrounds you? What do you give your energy to?* Most importantly – *how do you make the world better simply by being you?*

Your intentions are sacred architecture. Each one is a stone in the temple of your future. Write them with care. Bless them with prayer. These are not goals made from lack. They are songs from your wholeness.

When Richard Rudd speaks of the Gene Keys, he reminds us that our true potential is encoded in the very fabric of our DNA but is awakened through contemplation and intention. To say, "*I want to be healthy,*" is not enough. Say instead, "*I will tend to my vitality as a garden.*" Do not just say, "*I want to find love.*" Declare, "*I will become the kind of presence that love can recognize and join.*"

Embodied intentions are specific, felt, and generous. They are not about control, but co-creation. Each time you set an empowered intention; you are signaling to the universe: *I am ready. I am listening. I am aligned.* In this readiness, life begins to orchestrate around your clarity.

Intention is not a task for the intellect alone but a dialogue between soul and source. The more you return to intention, the more this shapes you. Speak aloud. Write on your walls. Let this live in your posture, breath, and rituals. An intention held without action is a dream deferred, but an intention honored daily becomes a magnetic field, quietly bending reality to meet your frequency.

Overcoming Inner Resistance

"The cave you fear to enter holds the treasure you seek." — Joseph Campbell

Every vision invites a dragon. Resistance is not a sign that you are on the wrong path but confirmation that you are on the edge of transformation. In many myths across cultures, the hero does not find the treasure without first encountering a beast. This is a metaphor of inner resistance.

Steven Pressfield names this force plainly: Resistance. The part of us that clings to the known, fears failure, and doubts the sacredness of our dreams. In the Dagara cosmology of West Africa, resistance is the initiator, not the enemy – which tests our sincerity, purifies our resolve, and strengthens our soul muscles.

Plotkin would call this the descent into soul. The moment where the ego no longer calls the shots, and we are asked to stand in our naked truth. Resistance reveals our edge. On this edge is where the real magic happens.

When you feel resistance, do not turn away. Create dialogue. Ask what is feared. Determine what is needed. Resistance is often just a younger part of us needing reassurance that we will not be abandoned. Wrap this in ritual. Breathe and dance with this opposing force. Write letters to your resistance, and then, walk forward anyway.

The embodied human does not wait for fear to disappear. They learn to move with all emotion. They let the trembling hand paint. They let the wobbly voice sing. This is courage – not the absence of resistance, but the commitment to our vision despite obstacles.

Resistance is often disguised as logic, telling us, "You are not ready," or "This is not the right time," when in truth, the threshold of your expansion is being guarded. Do not think of this as an enemy, but rather a sacred sentinel testing your readiness. When you push through – not with force, but with presence – you build the muscle of initiation. Each time you move toward your calling despite resistance, you create a new pattern, and eventually, the path that once felt blocked becomes a sacred current pulling you forward.

Becoming the Embodied Version of You

"The soul always knows what to do to heal. The challenge is to silence the mind." — Caroline Myss

There is a version of you that already exists – vibrant, grounded, awake. Your job now is not to become someone new, but to shed what is not you. Manly Hall said that, *"initiation is not about acquiring something new but is about awakening that which has always been within."*

To embody your vision is to dress in the skin of your soul. To walk, speak, eat, move, and rest as though you have already arrived. What does this version of you eat for breakfast? How do they treat their body? What do they say yes to, and what do they lovingly decline?

Indigenous elders often speak of walking in beauty. This means living in such a way that the Earth would be grateful for your footprints. That is the embodied you. You bless the land just by living with integrity. You speak truth even when inconvenient. You rest when needed, not as a luxury, but as spiritual practice.

To become the embodied version of yourself is to stop chasing and start listening. Your essence has always been speaking – through your longings, your grief, your dreams, your intuition. Embodiment means tuning into that quiet wisdom as your guide. This is not about reaching for a future version of yourself but living the emanation of who you are, now. Each breath you take in alignment becomes a vow to stay rooted in your path, not because of simplicity but because of authenticity.

The embodied self is not flawless but faithful – to truth, to joy, to service. Richard Rudd says, *"Your essence cannot be lost but can be forgotten."* This step is about remembering and reverencing that essence in daily rituals. When you falter – which you may – return to your breath, your body, your why. You are not here to perfect life. You are here to participate in sacred unfolding. As Huichol says, *"To walk the path with heart is to make of every step a prayer."*

In Step Twelve, we will turn our gaze outward. With a clear plan, a rooted self, and an embodied presence, we are now ready to help others remember what they, too, have forgotten. This is the ripple. This is the return.

Step Twelve: Becoming the Healer

Pass On with Love

"When you heal yourself, you heal your ancestors and your descendants. The medicine is not just for you but for the village." — Martin Prechtel

There is an ancient understanding whispered in the roots of all living things: *once you have tasted healing, you are now to become the medicine*. Step Twelve is a consecration, not a conclusion. A return to the village with fire in your hands and water in your voice. You do not arrive as a savior, but as one who has walked through the valley of shadows and returned bearing seeds. Now, your harvest is not just your own but is meant to feed others.

As Richard Rudd writes, *"The gift is not for you. The treasure moves through you."* In this final step, we embody what the Indigenous elders call the sacred responsibility of wisdom-keeping. Healing is not complete until shared. Just as mycelium weaves unseen networks beneath the soil, so too does your healed presence become an unseen blessing in the lives of others. You are no longer required to speak loudly. Your integrity is a potent frequency.

This step is a rite of passage. In the language of Bill Plotkin, you have crossed into the landscape of soul initiation. You are no longer merely healing – you are an emissary of healing. A living prayer.

You carry with you not just answers, but presence, reverence, and the embodied memory that transformation is possible. The medicine you hold is not a product, but a way of being. The world is waiting for your offering.

Now we explore how we carry this medicine forward – with humility, clarity, and love.

The GIVE Method

"The first peace, which is the most important, is that which comes within the souls of people when they realize their relationship, their oneness, with the universe and all powers." — Black Elk (Oglala Lakota Holy Man)

The GIVE Method is less a model than sacred agreement with life. Gratitude, Integrity, Vision, and Encouragement – four directions, four winds, four prayers that orient us in service. When we GIVE, we do not impose. We offer. We listen. We meet people not where we want them to be, but where they are. This is a conscious service.

Gratitude is our first medicine. When we serve others from a place of reverence – for their path, their wounds, their wisdom – we become mirrors of possibility rather than judges of failure. We see that people are broken but becoming. Every act of healing we offer must be seeded in thankfulness for the sacred story unfolding in each being.

Integrity means we live what we teach. As Manly Hall taught, the teacher who fails to embody their own doctrine is a hollow bell. Integrity asks us to be congruent in public and private. If we speak of nourishment, we must nourish ourselves. If we advocate for rest, we must rest.

Vision is what we hold on behalf of those who cannot yet see. In every traditional culture, elders are vision holders. They do not fix, they see. They remember the essence of a person even when that person has forgotten.

Encouragement is not a performance but a spiritual practice. In Andean tradition, *ayni* – sacred reciprocity – means offering what is most needed without expectation of return. A kind word, a blessing, a gesture of faith – these are initiations.

When we GIVE, we do not rescue. We invite. We hold space for others to reclaim their power.

Leading By Example

"We do not need leaders to tell us what to do. We need elders whose very presence reminds us who we are." — Martín Prechtel

The greatest teaching we will ever offer is the quality of our presence. People may forget our words, but they will never forget how we made them feel. To lead by example is to be a living transmission of the truth we now embody.

Leadership in the new paradigm is not about authority, but authenticity. This is not charisma, but coherence. The subtle magnetism of a life lived in alignment. Whether in the home, classroom, healing circle, or boardroom, your walk becomes your sermon.

In many Indigenous cultures, elders teach children not through punishment, but through modeling. The way an elder greets dawn, tends fire, speaks to the Earth – that is the curriculum. When you rise early to nourish your body with living food, when you listen deeply to another without distraction, when you dance in celebration of simply being alive – you are teaching.

Richard Rudd reminds us, *"The more you relax into who you truly are, the more others will remember who they are."* To lead by example is to become a mirror. Your joy, your boundaries, your forgiveness, your grief – all of this gives permission to others to be fully human.

This kind of leadership is not about having all the answers but becoming the kind of presence where the answers can arise. This is about walking in beauty, in service, and in love – and letting your life be the invitation.

Mentorship and Sacred Service

"The world in which you were born is just one model of reality. Other cultures are not failed attempts at being you; they are unique manifestations of the human spirit." — Wade Davis

To mentor is to midwife. You are not delivering anyone's soul – you are holding space as they remember how to birth themselves. Sacred service is not about hierarchy but kinship. This is about answering the soul's call to be useful, to participate in the healing of the whole.

Mentorship is rooted in humility and begins with the understanding that we are all still learning. As Parker Palmer says, *"The human soul does not want to be advised or fixed or saved but simply wants to be witnessed."* A true mentor does not invade but inquires. They ask questions that draw out the wisdom sleeping in another.

There is no single way to be a mentor. Some will guide through words. Others through art. Some will build schools; others will simply sit beside someone in silence. In the Dagara tradition, each elder has a medicine – some are storytellers, some are fire keepers, some are dreamers. Your service will be as unique as your fingerprint.

Sacred service is also ecological. As Plotkin suggests, true adulthood is defined not by what we consume, but by what we give back. The Earth is not asking us to save her, she is asking us to remember we belong. When we step into mentorship, we restore the web. We become one who tends to the future.

Whether through formal programs or quiet everyday acts, your service becomes an act of devotion. The objective is not about fixing the world but loving the world into the next becoming.

Sharing Your Light with the World

"The Elders say the world will be saved by the people who return to what is sacred." — Martín Prechtel

You are a lantern now. A firekeeper. This final step asks one thing of you: *Do not hide your light. Share your wisdom – not in grandeur, but in generosity.* As Lakota say, *"The sacred is not what is hidden from us. The sacred is what we give away."*

To share your light is to smile at strangers. To compost your sorrows into song. To speak truth even when your voice trembles. This is to live in such a way that others remember the beauty of being alive. Your story is medicine. Let your experiences be told.

Jim Henson once said, *"My hope still is to leave the world a bit better than when I got here."* This is noble, not naïve. We do not need to be famous to be impactful. We simply need to be faithful. Faithful to the daily act of choosing kindness. Faithful to beauty. Faithful to truth.

Indigenous wisdom teaches us that every being has a purpose, and every purpose is a gift to the whole. If you have healed even a little, then you have something to give. Whether through mentorship, activism, artistry, or quiet presence, your light is needed. Especially now.

As the twelfth step closes, a circle opens. You are not at the end; you are at the beginning of the next spiral. Go now, with gratitude in your bones, integrity in your spine, vision in your eyes, and encouragement in your voice.

You are the healer now. Not by perfection but by presence. Walk on.

"And let us not grow weary in doing good, for in due season, we shall reap, if we do not give up." – Galatians 6:9

Author's Epilogue: The Mirror Speaks Back

"Ironically, the lessons in our lives usually come from the advice we give others, not necessarily from books. So, listen carefully when you are sharing your wisdom with someone. The message is likely for you." – Zen to Zang

The idea for this book came to fruition during a dimly lit season of my life – a time when shadows whispered louder than hope. I stood on a threshold with a choice: surrender to despair or transmute my pain into purpose. I chose to write – not as an escape, but an offering. These pages became my altar. My practice. My prayer. They were the lanterns I lit to find my way home. In illuminating the path for others, I rediscovered my own light.

This book was first published in 2014 under the title *"Society's Anonymous: The True Twelve Steps to Recovery from What Brings Us Down."* Due to the circumstances in my life at that time, I never had an opportunity to promote or market the work. Therefore, these words remained stagnant and sealed. Eleven years later. I decided to revive the wisdom and revise the steps.

Each word you have read was born out of an alchemy – of transmuting grief into grace, confusion into clarity, and despair into a deeper kind of devotion. There were moments I did not know how to go on. When I felt like a cracked vessel carrying messages too sacred to hold. I kept writing, kept breathing, kept remembering that truth whispered from the edge of surrender. I had my daughter's smile etched in my memory, and the unshakable knowing that I had to rise for her, for myself, for anyone stumbling in the dark.

As I wrote, I felt more like a hollow bone than an author. Something ancient and luminous moved through me – a force wiser than I could ever be. At times, I felt Earth herself was speaking through my fingertips, calling us all back to wholeness, one sentence at a time. This book, while deeply personal, is not mine alone, but belongs to the collective soul of those who have wept quietly and kept going anyway. To all who have dared to live with an open heart in a hurting world.

In giving my voice to others, I found the strength to listen to my own. As Gabor Maté writes, *"The attempt to escape from pain, is what creates more pain."* By choosing to stay present through the discomfort, I unearthed something resilient, tender, and transformative. I realized that healing is not found in avoidance but lives in the raw places where we show up, again and again, even through pain.

I am a different man now than the one who began writing these chapters. I am more whole, more humbled, more human. If anything in these pages has helped lift even a small weight from your shoulders or reminded you of the beauty inside your own breath – then my task has been fulfilled. Thank you for taking this walk with me. Thank you for being brave enough to heal. Thank you, above all, for becoming the light you have been searching for.

With closing, this book becomes something else entirely. A mirror, a medicine bundle, a seed. I invite you to carry this, not as finished work, but as a living one. Let each lesson gather soil in your life, and bend and breathe with your becoming. Write your own words in the margins. Gift a copy to someone standing where you once stood. Let wisdom evolve. Allow your voice to become part of the echo. Stories, especially the healing ones, are meant to ripple outward, like prayers spoken into wind.

Living With a New Smile

"Smile, not because life has been perfect, but because you choose to show up with grace." — Doe Zantamata

There is a quiet strength in the smile that survives the storm. A kind of gentle rebellion. Not born from ease, but from resilience. Each time you soften your gaze toward yourself, you heal. Choosing presence over perfection, gratitude over judgment, helps radiate something sacred.

I once revived a houseplant others had written off as dead – not with science, but with belief, kindness, and a few tender words. I spoke to her gently. I trusted in her ability to return. She did. You, too, can return. Speak gently to your body. Water your soul with laughter. Let sunlight reach the parts of you that you have kept hidden. You are not broken. You are becoming.

In becoming, do not permit the world to harden your heart. *"Let your smile change the world, but do not let the world change your smile."* We live in a culture swirling with disconnection – anger, division, greed. When we hold our light steady, we do more than survive – we inspire.

As George Carlin said, *"Everyone smiles in the same language."* A smile crosses borders, melts fear, softens strangers. In a park filled with diverse faces and unfamiliar tongues, one smile can unify what words cannot. Nothing stops us from building that world – except our refusal to believe in the possibility.

Smiling is an act of faith, not an act of denial. This is your declaration, saying: *I still believe in beauty. I still believe in connection. I still believe in the human spirit's ability to rise.* When we smile, we open a channel that others also feel. Animals respond. Earth, too, receives.

Let your smile be medicine. A balm in chaotic places. A thread of warmth in a cold world. You may never know who needed to see, who was one breath away from giving up, until your presence reminded them of light.

In the Andean tradition, to walk with joy is to walk in the right relationship with Earth. Happiness is not a goal but a gift we give to the web of life when we choose to be fully present. Smiling is a ceremony. The world, dear soul, needs more ceremony.

Smiling is one of the most ancient forms of medicine – older than language, older than fire. Long before words were ever formed, our ancestors used the face, the breath, and the body to communicate warmth, openness, and trust. A smile is a gesture of peace that tells the nervous system: *I am safe here. I can soften. I can return.*

Some of the wisest elders I have met had faces carved with hardship – but their smiles lit up every room they entered. Their joy was not naïve but was earned. The kind of smile that had walked through death, disappointment, and doubt, and still chose to return to love. That is the kind of smile we cultivate here, not the smile of perfection, but the smile of presence.

You do not need to wait for life to be easy to smile. Smile now, while you are healing. Smile when the juice is blended just right. Smile at the sunrise. At the moonlight on your skin. At the small victories. At the strangers who forgot how radiant they are. Smile until your face remembers the shape of joy. Smile until your spirit remembers you were never meant to hide.

So, smile at your own reflection. Not because everything is perfect, but because you are still here – alive, becoming, remembering. This, alone, is reason enough.

Creating a Life You Were Meant to Live

"The privilege of a lifetime is to become who you truly are." — Carl Jung

Damian Mander is a former Australian Royal Navy clearance diver, and special operations military sniper. As a professional killer with SEEK & DESTROY tattooed across his chest, he is every bit intimidating. He has done twelve tours in Iraq and is literally *programmed to destroy*. He mentions in his TEDx speech how he knows exactly how many clicks of elevation are needed to take a headshot on a moving target from seven-hundred meters away.

What is most striking about Damian's speech is how his compassion and loving nature emerged even after all he has been through. While visiting Africa, he found purpose among chaos when he saw an elephant resting on her side with her face cut off – a vicious act of poaching.

At this moment, he asked himself a very important question: *Was he brave enough to give up his current way of living to save the lives of animals?* He decided to sell his homes, relocate to Africa, and exchange his previous life to start the *International Anti-Poaching Foundation* (iapf.org). His foundation is dedicated to protecting animals from poachers, while also guarding community assets and reducing habitat destruction.

He claims that through all his experiences, he has only performed one act of bravery that defines who he is. This was when he realized his purpose in life. He describes the decision to give up his former life to help animals by saying, *"There will never be separation between who I am, and what I do."* He created a life that aligns with his passions.

"The path to success is to take massive, determined action guided by integrity and love." – Thich Nhat Hanh

How many of us can honestly claim that there is no separation between who we are, and what we do? To live a life of depth and meaning, one that flows from our authentic essence, we must choose a path aligned with our deepest truths. In Damian's case, he spent years confronting destruction before uncovering his calling as a protector. Not a simple pivot, but a spiritual turning – from the mechanical precision of a sniper's eye to the soulful precision of heart-guided purpose.

These kinds of transformations do not happen overnight. They emerge from the compost of contradiction and the courage to ask the right questions. When we find the still voice inside that says, *"This is not who I truly am,"* and then listen – we can begin the work of realignment.

As Gabor Maté writes, *"When we suppress who we truly are in order to fit into the world, we create suffering – not just in ourselves, but in those around us."* Too often, we are praised for adapting rather than encouraged to embody our wholeness. We are groomed for performance, not purpose. We are conditioned to seek external approval while the flame of authenticity quietly dims. To reclaim our joy, our vitality, and our direction, we must remember who we are beneath the masks we were taught to wear. This requires radical honesty and a willingness to let go of the stories that no longer serve.

Decades may pass before we fully arrive at our calling. Some of us carry gifts we have not yet unwrapped. That is okay. Bob Ross spent twenty years in the United States Air Force, demanding perfection and discipline, before he vowed never to raise his voice again. The moment he put down the rigid tools of command and picked up a paintbrush, something within him softened.

Through soft-spoken brush strokes, he taught millions how to see beauty, embrace mistakes, and honor gentleness. To create a life that reflects the soul – to live in such a way that the truest parts of us are in motion.

The tennis legend, Arthur Ashe, once advised, *"To be successful, one has to start where they are, use what they have, and do what they can."* There is wisdom in this grounded simplicity. You do not need to figure anything out before taking your first step. The journey does not ask for perfection but presence, commitment, and a willingness to try. What matters most is that we begin – from wherever we are – and that we move in the direction of the life that is trying to emerge through us.

Let this be the threshold where you finally choose to live a life that is aligned with your nature. Allow this to be the moment where you soften into your authenticity and awaken to your dharma. There is no greater offering to the world than a life fully lived. There is no deeper healing than the kind that comes from being fully yourself.

Remember, just as Damian laid down his weapon to become a protector, and Ross laid down his drill sergeant voice to become a vessel of peace – you, too, are allowed to change course. To soften. To listen to the ache that lives beneath the armor. The question is no longer *"Who should I be?"* but *"What beauty is waiting to be born through me now?"*

When you align with that inner knowing, the world around you begins to shift. Synchronicities arise. Support finds you. Your breath deepens. Your smile returns. What once felt impossible begins to unfold – one soul-honoring step at a time.

The Ripple Effect of Happiness

"The light you give others guides you home." — Martín Prechtel

Happiness is a wave that travels further than we can see. Every time you choose to smile, extend kindness, share a nourishing word, or lend a hand, you activate a ripple. These waves of well-being reach people you may never meet, shifting their internal weather in ways you may not witness. Energy you emit has momentum. One act of compassion can soften hearts hardened by years of struggle, just as a single word of encouragement can reignite a dream that had nearly turned to ash.

In Indigenous traditions, health of an individual is intimately tied to health of a community. A joyful being is not seen as selfish but as a source of healing for the tribe. Becoming a beacon of joy makes you a steward of communal restoration. As Gabor Maté reminds us, *"The essence of trauma is disconnection from self."* The essence of healing is reconnection. When you choose happiness, you participate in mending the larger human soul.

Happiness becomes sacred when shared. When we laugh together, a kind of ancestral music plays across time. A child's giggle, an elder's gentle chuckle – these are echoes of a species remembering innocence. You have the power to bring these sounds into the world by honoring the spark from the great flame of life.

We are woven beings. What lifts one, lifts us all. Whether helping someone carry groceries, rescuing a wounded bird, planting a fruit tree in your neighborhood, or forgiving a stranger, these actions vibrate outward. The ripple effect is more than metaphor. We are referring to biology, emotion, and spirit bound together in movement. You matter. Your joy matters.

Awakening the New World Within

"The real voyage of discovery consists not in seeking new landscapes, but in having new eyes." — Marcel Proust

The most revolutionary act is not to change the world but to change ourselves so profoundly that the world no longer has power over our joy. Awakening the new world begins inside the silence of your own mind, in the breath you offer yourself when anxious, in the forgiveness you extend to your past self, and in compassion you grant others who are still asleep in theirs. This new world does not scream but hums quietly, rooted in integrity, aware of responsibility to the greater whole.

Inside you there is a realm vaster than any government, more intricate than any economy, more beautiful than any coastline. This realm is shaped by love, flowers in the soil of stillness, and thrives when nurtured with presence. You awaken this inner world not through external striving, but through internal surrender. Each moment you tend to your inner peace, you help midwife a world that thrives on cooperation, regeneration, and truth. This new world will not come through force but will arrive like dawn – gentle, gradual, undeniable.

Ancient Lakota understood that true vision arises not from seeking but from listening. Vision quests were not about fixing the world but attuning to Earth's pulse and remembering one's place in the sacred hoop. The new world within you longs for this same quiet alignment – a homecoming to the rhythm of all life. When you begin to live in reverence, the illusion of separation dissolves, and your inner world begins to mirror the harmony of creation.

Gabor Maté has said, *"We are not separate from the natural world; we are part of the breathing body."* To awaken this new world within is to become once again a lung of the Earth, breathing gently in rhythm with her. From this breath new realities will be born. Realities of unity. Of peace. Of fierce, compassionate presence. This is the power you carry now. This is the seed of the world yet to come.

To awaken the new world is to walk differently. You do not hustle for validation or seek status through conquest. You plant seeds. You notice birdsong. You slow your pace to the rhythm of breath and water. You speak less, but with more truth. In this shift, others begin to feel something ancient awakening inside themselves, too.

This is how a culture transforms: *not through mass instruction, but through millions of quiet revolutions unfolding in hearts across the planet.* One person unplugs from noise and listens. Another starts growing food. Someone else forgives their father. Another dances again after decades of silence. These changes ripple out like roots beneath soil – hidden but alive, reshaping the world from the ground up.

You do not need to save the world. You only need to awaken your part. As you tend to your inner garden, you create pathways for others to remember theirs. This is how Earth heals – not by demand, but by invitation. Not through pressure, but through presence. You are the world you wish to see. The revolution you have been waiting for is already within you.

A Message to the Future You

"The ancestors say: You are the dream of those who came before. Walk as if their prayers are beneath your feet."

To the version of you reading this years from now –may you never forget the courage to begin. There will be days when the path feels obscured, when the winds of the old world try to lure you back with comfort or conformity. You have touched a deeper truth. You know how to reclaim yourself, to rise from the ashes with clarity and strength. Let that knowing carry you forward. Trust in your evolution, even when wrapped in chaos.

The future you will thank the present you for choosing integrity over ease, kindness over judgment, and presence over distraction. The seeds you are planting now – seeds of resilience, awareness, and love – will blossom in the years to come. Keep showing up for your own unfolding. Keep listening to the quiet wisdom of your body. Keep walking barefoot on Earth and remembering where you came from. Above all, keep loving – fiercely, freely, without apology.

There will be those who misunderstand your journey. Let them. Not everyone will recognize the sacredness of the path you walk. You do not need to convince them. Continue choosing truth over illusion, connection over distraction, wonder over numbness. Each small act of beauty you live today becomes a steppingstone for the version of you reading this tomorrow.

When you forget – which you may – come back here. Return to these words, to your breath, to your intention. Remember: healing is not linear. Growth spirals. You are allowed to be soft, to pause, to cry, to celebrate. Life will offer you many mirrors. May you always choose the ones that reflect your radiance back to you.

The Final Word: Love as Action

"Action on behalf of life transforms. Because the relationship between self and the world is reciprocal, not a question of first getting enlightened or saved and then acting. As we work to heal the Earth, the Earth heals us." — Robin Wall Kimmerer

Love is a verb. A decision made moment by moment, to stand for life, to nurture what is sacred, and to choose connection even in the presence of conflict. Love as action means preparing food with reverence, speaking truth with gentleness, and showing up even when uncomfortable. The invisible scaffolding that holds the world upright.

This book, this journey, has not been about perfection but about love in motion. Love in practice. Love that composts the past and cultivates a future rooted in care. You are now a living embodiment of this love – not an idealized image, but a real human being who carries the medicine of presence. Let your hands heal. Let your words lift. Let your breath anchor you. Wherever you go, may your actions ripple out as prayers into the soil of tomorrow.

Love moves, soothes, and transforms. Like water shaping stone, love shifts the hardened places of this world into something softer, more receptive. Let your love be bold and challenge what is unjust. To reach into forgotten corners and remind the world that healing is possible, not through domination, but through devotion.

As Richard Rudd writes in The Gene Keys, *"Love is the only frequency that can heal the illusion of separation."* Let that be your legacy. Let your love be a salve on the aching body of this planet. May love rise not only in your heart, but in your feet, your voice, your choices. You are not here to wait for a better world. You are here to co-create, with love as your compass, and service as your vow.

Paradise (Reimagined)

We built paradise from the wild roots of imagination. Curiosity carved our paths, and the wisdom gathered along the way became sacred nourishment for the foundation. Ideas rose like timber beams; intention framed the walls. Love arched overhead like a sky-wide canopy, and compassion offered sheltering shade.

Struggle forged the support beams – each one tempered by fire, built to endure. Heartbreak sealed the windows so they would never shatter again. Education weatherproofed the roof, and knowledge flung open the panes, letting sunlight flood every room. Laughter dissolved all boundaries. Smiles erased the notion of limitation.

We replanted forests to nourish the land base. We grew food with reverence – organic, abundant, vibrant. Chemicals were no longer spoken in the language of harvest. Money was no longer mistaken for purpose. People danced with animals beneath the stars, and harmony became the atmosphere we breathed.

We remembered how to coexist. An ordinary world bloomed into the extraordinary. Souls climbed out of the abyss, still glowing with courage. The sun kissed our skin and whispered: *you are alive for a reason.*

As awakened individuals, we honored our purpose and created this.

The Best Teacher I Never Knew I Needed

They say every teacher leaves an imprint, but some carve something deeper – a path, a light, a turning point. This is the story of such a teacher and of a boy who taught her everything she thought she already knew.

Ms. Hartley had been teaching fifth grade for nearly a decade. She believed she had seen all – the shining stars, class clowns, quiet ones who surprised you, and those who made you question why you ever chose this profession. That fall, a boy named Eli walked into her classroom, and nothing would ever be the same.

Eli was small for his age. He rarely spoke. His clothes clung to him like afterthoughts, his hair often unbrushed, and his eyes downcast. He rarely turned in homework, and when he did, the assignment was often smudged or incomplete. Other children noticed. Some teased. Ms. Hartley, though well-meaning, found herself frustrated. She tried to remain impartial, but something about Eli's silence made her uncomfortable. She assumed the worst.

She was able to see behind the veil after reviewing his file during winter break. In first grade, Eli was described as imaginative and bright, *"a spark in every corner of the room."* Second grade noted a shift: *his mother had been diagnosed with a serious illness.* Third grade reported chronic absenteeism – *his mother had passed away.* By fourth grade, the notes said, *"Withdrawn. Does not engage. Father struggles with addiction. Home visits are unsuccessful."*

Ms. Hartley closed the file, her hands trembling. Her throat burned with shame. She had failed him, not academically, but emotionally. She returned to school in January different. Her lessons stayed the same, but her way of seeing did not. She began to greet Eli each morning with genuine warmth. She asked about his interests. She kept snacks in her drawer and saved him a seat at the front. When Valentine's Day came, he handed her a card. Just a folded piece of notebook paper with the words *"thank you for seeing me."* She knew she would never be the same.

Over time, Eli opened. His eyes lifted. He began to participate. When he laughed for the first time in class, everyone was startled, including himself. He brought in a story he wrote about a fox who did not fit in, but who saved the forest in the end. Ms. Hartley read his work aloud. The class clapped. Eli beamed.

Years passed. Notes arrived in the mail. First from high school: *"I made honor roll. Thank you for making me believe I could."* Then college: *"Majoring in literature. Thinking of teaching."* Finally, an invitation. A wedding.

She went. She wore the same necklace Eli once saw her wear on the day he read his story aloud – the day he said later, that made him want to speak again. When the vows were said, and the night was winding down, he found her. They embraced. Eli whispered, *"You saved my life."* Ms. Hartley, with tears in her eyes, whispered back, *"No, Eli. You saved mine."*

Some teachers mark papers. Others mark souls. This story is about both.

A Vow to the Life You Were Meant to Live

Promise yourself. To be so aligned with your purpose that nothing disturbs the sanctuary of your mind. To speak of healing, happiness, and harmony to every soul you encounter. To help others remember their sacred worth by recognizing the divine within them.

Promise yourself. To find the light behind every shadow and make your vision of joy become your reality. To believe in the highest within you, work in service of the good, and expect beauty to rise from the ashes. To celebrate the victories of others with the same wonder you reserve for your own. To leave behind the echoes of regret and walk forward into the horizon of your becoming.

Promise yourself. To wear the smile that touches hearts, and offer this freely to humans, animals, plants, and stones. To be so devoted to your personal evolution that judgment has no place in your presence. To become too rooted for fear, too humble for pride, too conscious for confusion, and too alive for apathy.

Promise yourself. To know your worth not in words, but in the way you live, the way you love, and the legacy you leave. To trust, with unwavering faith, that life moves in your favor when you move in alignment with the best that lives within you.

Twelve Steps to Sacred Self-Care

A vow to yourself, for the life you were meant to live

- Let go of what does not feel true to your soul.
- Speak clearly, kindly, and with unwavering honesty.
- Release the need to please – your peace matters more.
- Trust the whispers of your inner knowing.
- Speak of yourself as you speak to someone you love.
- Hold your dreams like sacred seeds – always water them.
- Let *"No"* be a sentence that protects your boundaries.
- Let *"Yes"* be a portal that opens to joy and alignment.
- Treat yourself with the gentleness you long for as a child.
- Surrender what you cannot control – with grace.
- Step away from the fires of gossip, chaos, and smallness.
- Return to love, again and again.

– A Living Proverb

Children Reflect the World We Create

If children live with criticism, they learn to shrink. With blame, they learn to hide. In ridicule, they learn to silence their gifts. Surrounded by shame, they learn to fear their own voice. In the presence of punishment, they learn that love must be earned.

Contrary to this, if children live with presence, they learn they are worth your time. Familiar with curiosity, they learn that questions are sacred. Knowing consistency, they learn that trust is real. Experiencing forgiveness, they learn to begin again. Wondering, they know the world is alive.

When praised, they learn to believe in their gifts. If met with compassion, they learn to soften in the face of pain. Given respect, they learn to value their place in the circle. When they are heard, they learn to speak with purpose. If loved simply for existing, they learn to love themselves without condition.

Children are not clay to be molded, they are gardens to be nurtured. They bloom not by force, but by sunlight, water, and the space to grow. What they learn from how we live; they will carry into the world we are yet becoming.

About the Author

Jesse Jacoby is a dedicated father, expressionist, and advocate for compassion, equanimity, and purity. He expends energy adventuring in forests, creating, learning, playing, and writing.

Jesse is the founder and CEO of Soulspire: The Healing Playground (*soulspire.com*). This is a biohacking and purification center with locations near Lake Tahoe in Truckee, CA, and in Nevada City, CA.

He is also the founder of the Global School of Purification (*schoolofpurity.com*), which is an educational course instructing how to regenerate health in the body and providing certifications for global purification specialists.

Additionally, Jesse is a co-founder of Substance Shield (substanceshield.com), which is an organic, wild-crafted supplement line for replenishing the body before and after substance use.

Jesse is the author of The Raw Cure: Healing Beyond Medicine (1st & 2nd Editions), The Way Knows: Trusting Divine Orchestration, Where Galaxies Kiss the Earth, The High Life, Windsdom: Wisdom from the Wind, Sovereign Biology, Modern Human Conditions, You Are Not Powerless, Gaia Speaks, Eating Plant-Based: The New Health Paradigm, and My Quest to Conquer What Matters. He also published a series of children's books.

Jesse@soulspire.com

Bibliography

Foreword:

Maté, Gabor. *In the Realm of Hungry Ghosts: Close Encounters with Addiction*. North Atlantic Books, 2010.

Centers for Disease Control and Prevention. "Suicide Data and Statistics." *CDC*, 2023, www.cdc.gov/suicide/facts/index.html. Accessed 22 Mar. 2025.

Zen to Zang. *Zen to Zang: Timeless Wisdom for Modern Living*. Self-published, 2021.

Introduction:

Maté, Gabor. *When the Body Says No: Exploring the Stress-Disease Connection*. Vintage Canada, 2019.

Chopra, Deepak. *Perfect Health: The Complete Mind Body Guide*. Harmony Books, 2001.

Gundry, Steven R. *The Plant Paradox: The Hidden Dangers in "Healthy" Foods That Cause Disease and Weight Gain*. Harper Wave, 2017.

Young, Robert O., and Shelley Redford Young. *The pH Miracle: Balance Your Diet, Reclaim Your Health*. Grand Central Life & Style, 2010.

Seneff, Stephanie. "Glyphosate, Pathways to Modern Diseases." *Entropy*, vol. 15, no. 4, 2013, pp. 1416–1463.

Opening Chapters:

Centers for Disease Control and Prevention. "Suicide Data and Statistics." *CDC*, 2023, https://www.cdc.gov/suicide/facts/data.html. Accessed 31 Mar. 2025.

Centers for Disease Control and Prevention. "FastStats - Depression." *CDC*, 2023, https://www.cdc.gov/nchs/fastats/depression.htm. Accessed 31 Mar. 2025.

National Institute of Mental Health. "Suicide." *NIMH*, 2023, https://www.nimh.nih.gov/health/statistics/suicide. Accessed 31 Mar. 2025.

Step I:

Anonymous. "Inflammation is the root of all disease..." *Traditional Holistic Proverb*. n.d.

de Mello, Anthony. *Awareness: The Perils and Opportunities of Reality*. Image, 1992.

Dyer, Wayne. *Your Erroneous Zones*. Harper Paperbacks, 2001.

Emerson, Ralph Waldo. *Self-Reliance and Other Essays*. Dover Publications, 1993.

Esselstyn, Caldwell B. *Prevent and Reverse Heart Disease*. Avery, 2007.

Jung, Carl. *Modern Man in Search of a Soul*. Harcourt, 1933.

Kingsford, Jana. *Unjuggled: The Art of Having It All Without Doing It All*. Elevate, 2018.

Lennon, John. "Count your age by friends, not years..." *Inspirational Quotes by John Lennon*.

Maté, Gabor. *In the Realm of Hungry Ghosts: Close Encounters with Addiction*. North Atlantic Books, 2010.

Nin, Anaïs. *The Diary of Anaïs Nin*. Harcourt, various volumes.

Vanzant, Iyanla. *Acts of Faith: Daily Meditations for People of Color*. Fireside, 1993.

Weller, Francis. *The Wild Edge of Sorrow: Rituals of Renewal and the Sacred Work of Grief*. North Atlantic Books, 2015.

Step II:

Easwaran, Eknath, translator. *The Upanishads*. Nilgiri Press, 2007.

Frankl, Viktor E. *Man's Search for Meaning*. Beacon Press, 2006.

McKenna, Terence. Quoted in "Terence McKenna: Nature Loves Courage." *Psychedelic Science Review*, www.psychedelicreview.com/terence-mckenna-nature-loves-courage/. Accessed [insert date].

Maharshi, Ramana. Quoted in "Correcting oneself is correcting the whole world..." *Quotefancy*, www.quotefancy.com. Accessed [insert date].

Stone, W. Clement. Quoted in *The Success System That Never Fails*. Prentice Hall, 1962.

Step III:

Hanh, Thich Nhat. *Peace Is Every Step: The Path of Mindfulness in Everyday Life*. Bantam, 1991.

Twain, Mark. Quoted in *Mark Twain's Notebook*. Harper & Row, 1935.

Hippocrates. Quoted in Wootton, David. *Bad Medicine: Doctors Doing Harm Since Hippocrates*. Oxford UP, 2006.

Franklin, Jentezen. *Fasting: Opening the Door to a Deeper, More Intimate, More Powerful Relationship with God*. Charisma House, 2008.

"Soulspire: The Healing Playground." Soulspire, www.soulspire.com. Accessed 01 Apr. 2025.

"PEMF Therapy: What Is It & How Does It Work?" *Healthline*, www.healthline.com/health/pemf-therapy. Accessed 01 Apr. 2025.

"Infrared Sauna Therapy Benefits." *Cleveland Clinic*, my.clevelandclinic.org. Accessed 01 Apr. 2025.

"Lymphatic Drainage Massage: What You Should Know." *Medical News Today*, www.medicalnewstoday.com. Accessed 01 Apr. 2025.

"Juice Fasting and Detoxification." *Gerson Institute*, www.gerson.org. Accessed 01 Apr. 2025.

Step IV:

McLester, James. "Nutrition and Health." *Journal of the American Medical Association*, 1939, pp. 1839–1843.

Hawkins, David R. *Power vs. Force: The Hidden Determinants of Human Behavior*. Hay House, Inc., 2014.

Baranski, Marcin, et al. "Higher Antioxidant and Lower Cadmium Concentrations and Lower Incidence of Pesticide Residues in Organically Grown Crops: A Systematic Literature Review and Meta-Analyses." *British Journal of Nutrition*, vol. 112, no. 5, 2014, pp. 794–811.

Koeth, Rachel A., et al. "Trimethylamine N-Oxide (TMAO), Diet, and Cardiovascular Risk." *Current Atherosclerosis Reports*, vol. 18, no. 6, 2016, pp. 1–7.

Samsel, Anthony, and Stephanie Seneff. "Glyphosate's Suppression of Cytochrome P450 Enzymes and Amino Acid Biosynthesis by the Gut Microbiome: Pathways to Modern Diseases." *Entropy*, vol. 15, no. 4, 2013, pp. 1416–1463.

Xu, Pengcheng, et al. "Fructose-Induced Neuroinflammation via P2X7 Receptor Activation Results in Hippocampal Neuronal Apoptosis." *Molecular Neurobiology*, vol. 59, 2022, pp. 2722–2737.

Zhou, Bin, et al. "Dietary Sugar Intake and Depression: A Meta-Analysis of Observational Studies." *Frontiers in Nutrition*, vol. 10, 2023, pp. 1170342.

Szent-Györgyi, Albert. *The Living State: With Observations on Cancer*. Academic Press, 1972.

Rosinger, Asher Y., et al. "Dehydration and Depression: An Analysis from the National Health and Nutrition Examination Survey (NHANES)." *World Journal of Psychiatry*, vol. 8, no. 1, 2018, pp. 50–59.

Step V:

Chevalier, Gaétan, and Stephen T. Sinatra. "Effects of Mindful Walking in Nature on Psychological Well-being: A Randomized Controlled Trial." *Frontiers in Psychology*, vol. 11, 2020, p. 2262.

Lee, Ka-Man, and Ravi Maheswaran. "Nature and Health: The Influence of Nature Exposure on Health Outcomes." *Environmental Research*, vol. 155, 2017, pp. 275–284.

Li, Qing. "Effect of Forest Bathing Trips on Human Immune Function." *Environmental Health and Preventive Medicine*, vol. 15, no. 1, 2010, pp. 9–17.

Marshall, Jane. "Yoga and the Nervous System: A Pathway to a Healthier Life." *Journal of Bodywork and Movement Therapies*, vol. 22, no. 1, 2018, pp. 263–268.

Ober, Clint, Stephen T. Sinatra, and Gaetan Chevalier. "Earthing: Health Implications of Reconnecting the Human Body to the Earth's Surface Electrons." *Journal of Environmental and Public Health*, vol. 2012, 2012, pp. 1–8.

Step VI:
Ikeda, Daisaku. *Unlocking the Mysteries of Birth and Death*. Middleway Press, 2003.
Wooden, John. *Wooden: A Lifetime of Observations and Reflections On and Off the Court*. McGraw-Hill, 1997.
Mandela, Nelson. *Long Walk to Freedom: The Autobiography of Nelson Mandela*. Little, Brown and Company, 1994.
Holmes, Oliver Wendell. *The Autocrat of the Breakfast-Table*. Phillips, Sampson, and Company, 1858.

Step VII:
Rohn, Jim. *The Five Major Pieces to the Life Puzzle*. Jim Rohn International, 1991.
Twain, Mark. *Following the Equator: A Journey Around the World*. American Publishing Company, 1897.
Nelson, Willie. *The Tao of Willie: A Guide to the Happiness in Your Heart*. Gotham Books, 2006.
Mallary, Dominic Owen. *Selected Writings and Letters*. Self-published, 2008.

Step VIII:
Hanh, Thich Nhat. *Being Peace*. Parallax Press, 1987.
Krishnamurti, Jiddu. *Think on These Things*. HarperCollins, 1964.
Marley, Bob. "Redemption Song." *Uprising*, Island Records, 1980.
Roosevelt, Theodore. *Theodore Roosevelt: An Autobiography*. Macmillan, 1913.
Woolf, Virginia. *A Room of One's Own*. Harcourt, Inc., 1929.

Step IX:
Bhagavad Gita. *The Bhagavad Gita*. Penguin Books, 2003.
Richard Rudd. *The Gene Keys: Unlocking the Higher Purpose Hidden in Your DNA*. Ouroboros Press, 2013.
Orlando A. Battista. *The Power to Influence People*. Prentice-Hall, 1959.
Virginia Woolf. *A Room of One's Own*. Harcourt, Inc., 1929.

Step X:
Chopra, Deepak. *The Book of Secrets: Unlocking the Hidden Dimensions of Your Life*. Harmony Books, 2006.
Hall, Manly P. *The Secret Teachings of All Ages*. TarcherPerigee, 1996.
Meade, Michael. *The Genius Myth*. GreenFire Press, 2016.
Plotkin, Bill. *Nature and the Human Soul: Cultivating Wholeness and Community in a Fragmented World*. New World Library, 2008.
Rudd, Richard. *The Gene Keys: Unlocking the Higher Purpose Hidden in Your DNA*. O Books, 2013.
Somé, Malidoma Patrice. *The Healing Wisdom of Africa: Finding Life Purpose Through Nature, Ritual, and Community*. Tarcher/Putnam, 1998.
Rumi. *The Essential Rumi*. Edited by Coleman Barks, HarperOne, 2004.

Step XI:
Whyte, David. *Crossing the Unknown Sea: Work as a Pilgrimage of Identity*. Riverhead Books, 2001.
Plotkin, Bill. *Soulcraft: Crossing into the Mysteries of Nature and Psyche*. New World Library, 2003.
Hall, Manly P. *The Secret Teachings of All Ages*. TarcherPerigee, 2003.
Rudd, Richard. *Gene Keys: Unlocking the Higher Purpose Hidden in Your DNA*. O Books, 2013.
Pressfield, Steven. *The War of Art: Break Through the Blocks and Win Your Inner Creative Battles*. Black Irish Entertainment LLC, 2012.

Step XII:
Hall, Manly P. *The Secret Teachings of All Ages*. TarcherPerigee, 2003.
Henson, Jim. *It's Not Easy Being Green: And Other Things to Consider*. Hyperion, 2005.
Palmer, Parker J. *A Hidden Wholeness: The Journey Toward an Undivided Life*. Jossey-Bass, 2004.
Plotkin, Bill. *Soulcraft: Crossing into the Mysteries of Nature and Psyche*. New World Library, 2003.
Rudd, Richard. *Gene Keys: Unlocking the Higher Purpose Hidden in Your DNA*. O Books, 2013.

The Holy Bible, New International Version. Zondervan, 2011. (for Galatians 6:9)

Closing Sections:

Doe Zantamata. *Happiness in Your Life*. Compendium Inc., 2012.

Thich Nhat Hanh. *How to Relax*. Parallax Press, 2015.

Jiddu Krishnamurti. *Think on These Things*. HarperCollins, 1994.

George Carlin. *Brain Droppings*. Hyperion, 1997.

Gabor Maté. *The Myth of Normal: Trauma, Illness, and Healing in a Toxic Culture*. Avery, 2022.

Richard Rudd. *Gene Keys: Unlocking the Higher Purpose Hidden in Your DNA*. O Books, 2013.

The Healing Playground

Soulspire is a next-generation biohacking, detoxification, and purification facility with locations in Truckee, CA and Nevada City, CA. We provide cutting-edge therapeutic & restorative services designed to support deep personal transformation.

Through a fusion of ancient wisdom, modern technology, and synergistic protocols – from oxygen to red light, colon hydrotherapy, frequency therapies, healing with voltage and beyond – we are redefining the meaning of wellness in the modern world.

Substance Shield
Ally of the Aftermath

Substance Shield is a botanical supplement line born from the wisdom of The High Life, a guide for conscious living in a chemically saturated world. Our products exist to support the body's resilience before and after exposure to substances, offering tools of renewal, not judgment. Whether facing pharmaceutical fallout, recreational recovery, or environmental residue, our mission is to replenish what modern life strips away.

Every formula is organic, vegan, wild-harvested, and crafted from whole foods, roots, and ancient botanicals designed to support detoxification pathways, restore depleted micronutrients, and aid in cellular resilience.

Our Mission

- To honor the human experience without shame.

- To offer nourishment to those navigating a chemically compromised world.

- To protect the body's brilliance through nature's most intelligent pharmacy.

- To replenish what substances diminish, without ever promoting their use.

- To be the shield when the soul forgets we have one.

We believe everyone deserves to recover their clarity, reclaim their vitality, and rise stronger after the storm. Whether you have danced with the edge or been caught in the crossfire, Substance Shield is your ally of the aftermath.

www.substanceshield.com
Instagram: @substanceshield

www.ingramcontent.com/pod-product-compliance
Lightning Source LLC
Chambersburg PA
CBHW081507040426
42446CB00017B/3425